Th **D1231698** ory

a-12-18

THE DIZZY DEAN STORY

In the long history of baseball, no player ever had more color and excitement than Dizzy Dean, spectacular pitcher for the famous St. Louis Cardinals of the 1930's and now a sportscaster for a national radio-TV network. His brilliant career was cut short by a foot injury and a sore arm, yet he won a place in baseball's Hall of Fame. In 1934 he established a modern National League record of thirty games won in a single season; no other pitcher in baseball has since matched this achievement.

Books by Milton J. Shapiro

THE SAL MAGLIE STORY
JACKIE ROBINSON OF THE BROOKLYN DODGERS
THE WARREN SPAHN STORY
THE ROY CAMPANELLA STORY
THE PHIL RIZZUTO STORY
THE MEL OTT STORY
THE WILLIE MAYS STORY
THE GIL HODGES STORY
THE HANK AARON STORY
A BEGINNER'S BOOK OF SPORTING GUNS AND HUNTING
MICKEY MANTLE: Yankee Slugger
THE WHITEY FORD STORY
THE DIZZY DEAN STORY

The Dean boys, l. to r.—Dizzy, Paul, Elmer.

Dizzy shuts out Reds to cinch National League pennant (1934).

Dizzy bears down on Tigers in first game of World Series (1934).

Dizzy horns in on the band (1934).

Manager Frisch congratulates Dizzy on his shutout victory over Tigers in deciding game of World Series (1934).

Dizzy and Paul, star brother pitching combination for the Cardinals (1935).

Dizzy with Ford Frick, President of the National League (1938).

Dizzy shows his running skill in game w Brooklyn (1939).

Dizzy works on his farm in Lancaster, Texas (1943).

Dizzy telecasting Yankee-Dodger game (1950).

Mr. and Mrs. Dean with picture of his Hall of Fame plaque (1953).

Two former baseball stars, now both spor announcers—Dizzy Dean and Pee Wee Rees (1961).

THE
DIZZY DEAN
STORY

●●●●●●●●●●●●●●●●●●●

by
MILTON J. SHAPIRO

JULIAN MESSNER, INC.   NEW YORK

Published by Julian Messner, Inc.
8 West 40th Street, New York 18

Published simultaneously in Canada
by The Copp Clark Publishing Co. Limited

Photographs used with the permission of
Wide World Photos and United Press International.

19366

Printed in the United States of America
Library of Congress Catalog Card No. 63–8640

*With grateful acknowledgment
to Bill Carr for his help in
the preparation of this book*

THE DIZZY DEAN STORY

1 ••••••

In the clapboard, one-room schoolhouse that served the Ozark town of Chickalah in the spring of 1919, schoolmaster Ralph Dennis faced young Jay Hanna Dean one morning.

"Jay Hanna," he said, his voice a pleasant Arkansas drawl, "I'm sorry to say your readin' hasn't improved hardly at all. Eight-year-old boy like you should be on his third reader by now, but you can hardly get through the second. You been readin' aloud at home to your father like I tol' you to?"

Jay Hanna Dean shuffled his bare feet on the hardwood floor and looked up at the schoolmaster. "Pa don' care much to hear what's in the second reader, Mr. Dennis." His eyebrows knitted in a frown. "Cain't say I care much to hear it m'self, to tell the whole truth."

The youngsters in the classroom giggled. Ralph Dennis forced a stern look upon his face. "Come up front, Jay Hanna," he said. When the boy stood in front of the class the schoolmaster drew a circle on the blackboard, then took the boy's arm and led him forward. "You will stand with your nose in that circle till school is over today, Jay Hanna. Perhaps it will help impress upon you the value of learning your lessons."

Jay Hanna Dean shrugged and scratched his head absently. It wasn't the first time this punishment had been given him; it was one of Mr. Dennis's favorites. That and the hickory stick, of course. As he stood there, nose pressed against the slate, he vaguely heard the sniffs and titters of his classmates, but they didn't bother him. He had the faculty, at such moments, of removing his mind from his surroundings and settling it elsewhere, someplace where things were more pleasant, where there were no second readers or sums to baffle him, no spelling bees to make him look foolish.

Right now his mind was among the mountains. There was Pa, leading the way, with big brother Elmer right behind, then him and little Paul trailing after, scrambling over the rocks and crashing through the pine boughs. They were hot after a bear, or maybe treeing a possum, their old coon hound yipping along the trail. Or maybe they were just sitting on a big log throwing rocks at squirrels. He liked that best of all, throwing rocks at squirrels. Pa said he had the powerfulest and straightest throwing arm he ever did see in a boy his age. It made him feel proud when Pa said that, and it made him try even harder to throw straight and strong, to search the floor of the forest for the smoothest, roundest stones to throw, because they were the best and the easiest to control.

In this way did the mind of Jay Hanna Dean wander

that spring morning, enabling him to escape the class-room that burdened him, the punishment that hu-miliated him—though he would never have admitted to the latter. When the bell finally clanged at the end of the schoolday he left with the others, not looking directly at any of them or schoolmaster Dennis. He ignored the calls of his friends to play, but walked firmly and de-terminedly over the fields toward the frame shack that was his home. As he approached, he saw his father, shoul-ders hunched, leaning heavily into a plow. He called out to him, and waved, then threaded his way carefully through a thickly planted cotton field.

Monroe Dean straightened from his plow and mopped his face with a big red handkerchief. "How'd she go in school today, boy?" he said when his son reached him.

Jay Hanna curled his toes into the rich earth, freshly turned, feeling its coolness. He looked down at his feet, then up, straight into his father's eyes.

"Pa," he said, "I ain't goin' back to that school no more."

His father looked at him quizzically for a moment, then sighed. "If your Ma were alive it might have been different. She set some store by book larnin'. But you done as good as your brother Elmer did, and I guess that's good enough. You can read and write some, and there's plenty around here cain't do none of either." He clapped his son on the shoulder. "Go in the house and get you somethin' to eat. Then see if you can find your brother Paul. He's wandered off somewheres."

11

Monroe Dean would have wanted it to be otherwise. Like so many Ozark mountain men he had some vague dream of better things—better for himself, better for his sons. Stories were always making the rounds of the hills about some sharecropper's son going down to Little Rock to "larn the law" or maybe become a schoolteacher or local politician. Monroe Dean dreamed about this, but he had no idea how to go about turning such a dream into reality. Instead, like so many of his kind, poor, rootless, uneducated, he waited for some miracle to take place—something, he knew not what, that would get him a piece of land of his own or a little business or lift one of his sons from the rut of sharecropping poverty and put him on the path toward a richer, fuller life.

But when Jay Hanna was only three years old and Paul barely a year, his wife died. Good woman that she was, she at least made them a family and as a family they had reason to hope, to dream, to plan. Often they would talk about "putting something by" to educate one of the boys, send him north to one of the bigger towns like Dardanelle or Russellville, where there was a real high school.

But when his wife died, Monroe Dean knew he would never have anything but a dream, that he and his sons were destined to sharecrop away their lives, plowing and hoeing and picking cotton on other men's land. He didn't see how it could ever be otherwise.

As for Jay Hanna, he gave no thought to his future. Free of the schoolwork he dreaded, he drifted into his early teens a comparatively happy, carefree boy. Barefoot and in his one good pair of overalls, he trailed after his father from farm to farm, crossing the border into Texas occasionally to pick cotton, climbing into the Ozarks after fresh venison, fishing the turbulent streams when there was no meat.

It was a gypsy life. In two battered old Model T Fords —Elmer driving one, Mr. Dean the other—they wandered from county to county, taking work when and as they found it, playing when it suited them.

Play, for the Deans, was mostly baseball.

In his youth Monroe Dean had developed a love for the game. He knew of the legends surrounding such baseball greats as John McGraw, Tris Speaker, Grover Cleveland Alexander and Babe Ruth. He dreamed, from time to time, of how it would be, playing professional baseball. In his teens he began to play in the pickup games that flourished around the small towns of the South, setting himself up as a pitcher. He developed enough skill at it to earn a little money week ends playing with several small semipro teams. But an early marriage and the necessity to earn a living swiftly killed any pretensions he might have had toward continuing in baseball. Itinerant farming and sharecropping were a seven-day-a-week proposition, leaving no time for baseball.

Now, in the vagabond existence he led with his sons, he found time for baseball again. Elmer, the oldest, seemed to have little inclination for the game, but Jay Hanna and Paul took to their father's instruction eagerly. Baseball for them began in some forgotten field in Ar-

13

kansas with a hoe handle for a bat and strips of tape around an apple core as a ball. First the boys took turns batting with the hoe handle as their father pitched. They flailed away gleefully with the homemade bat, while brother Elmer fielded the ragged "baseball."

Then Mr. Dean showed them how to pitch, how to grip the ball. "Now watch how I gives it a windup afore I throw." Then, grunting as he threw, "See how I put my shoulder in it, an' watch how I flip my wrist."

"There's not only fast balls, which is thrown straight," he said one day, "but now I wanna teach you how to throw inshoots and outshoots. Some folks call 'em curves. Of course, it ain't easy with a li'l ol' ball like this, but someday, when we can save up a little money, we'll buy us a real baseball and I'll show you. But fer now, you hold the ball like this, see," he said, demonstrating a grip on the taped ball, "and just as you let go the ball, you put a little snap an' roll in your wrist, like this." And he showed them how.

As Monroe Dean had realized, it was difficult to throw a true curve with the soft, makeshift ball they used. Daily practice, however, instilled the technique in his sons' throwing habits; and when the time did come later that they could afford to buy an old regulation baseball in a nearby town, both Paul and Jay Hanna, still barely in their teens, threw passable curves.

Whenever they could find the time and the opportunity, the Deans would park the old Fords and take part in a pickup baseball game. It was not long before the Dean trio—father and two young sons—were known on the cotton-picking circuit as a valuable addition to a pickup team, especially when, as was sometimes the case, the game was played for money. The stakes were only a half dollar or a dollar for the game, or, as they were often set, "a nickel a man." But the fifteen or thirty cents the Deans won this way—and they won far more often than they lost—meant the equivalent of nearly a day's pay for a man picking cotton.

It was during one of these pickup games that Jay Hanna became friendly with another Arkansas boy named Jerome Herman. Some months after their first meeting, when the Deans passed through the same town, Jay Hanna learned that his friend had died.

"Pa," he said to his father, "I reckon that poor mother must be mighty sad to lose Jerome Herman. She didn't have but one boy. I think maybe she'd feel better if I change my name to Jerome Herman. That way it'll be almost like she still had him around."

Monroe Dean scratched his head. "It sure seems like a strange idea, Jay Hanna, but if that's what you want, why you just go ahead and call yourself Jerome Herman. It'll take some gettin' used to for me and your brothers, but we'll try."

So Jay Hanna became in time Jerome Herman, though his original name lingered long into the years when he became famous, causing confusion in many of baseball's record books.

THE DIZZY DEAN STORY

2 ••••••

A lone jalopy creaked and wheezed its way along the dirt road that led into San Antonio, Texas, leaving a trail of dust behind to cloud the clear November air. Jerome Herman Dean, as he now called himself, sixteen years old, tall and gangly, sat behind the wheel, his father beside him, brother Paul in the back seat. Elmer, in the other jalopy, had been missing a week now, separated from his family by a long freight train that had come between the two cars at a crossing. The Deans, mountain men and stolid, were not overly concerned.

"Where you think Elmer might be at now?" Jerome said, turning his head to address his father.

Mr. Dean shrugged, puffing contentedly at a corncob pipe. "Workin', I hope, wherever he be at," he said after a moment. "Don't fret none, boy, Elmer's big enough to take care of hisself. He'll meet up with us one of these days and we'll all be together again."

"Sure funny though," Paul said from the back seat, "the way that ol' freight cut Elmer off. Like to near cut the front of his jalopy off, with him racing to get across the track an' catch up with us!"

16

Jerome laughed. "Haw! I'd sure like to see ol' Elmer's face right then. Bet he thought we'd be waitin' fer him too when that freight went by."

Monroe Dean snorted. "Bet that freight took fifteen minutes to go by if it took a second," he said. "Musta stretched from here to Texarkana. Wouldn't wait that long for President Coolidge hisself, no less Elmer."

The jalopy bumped its way across a rough crossroad, then Jerome twisted the wheel and headed down a smoother side road that led along a high wire fence studded with signs reading: "U.S. Government Military Reservation. Authorized Persons Enter Only."

"Too bad, maybe, I weren't never in the Army," Monroe Dean mused. "Might be gettin' a nice pension now, or one of them easy guvamint jobs they give out to veterans. Might even of stayed in, become one of them thirty-year men, got myself stationed here at Fort Sam Houston. Ain't too bad a life, bein' a sojer, if you don't mind bein' ordered around all the time."

"Yeah," Paul said, "but maybe you would of been killed in the war, too, and then where would me and Jerome and Elmer be?"

"Livin' good off'n federal money, that's where. But shucks, you know I wouldn' of got killed. Mountain men are too smart to get killed. You heard about that Sergeant York, didn't you? Killed all them Germans and never a scratch? Mountain man, same as us."

"Know somethin', Pa?" Jerome said, "I think maybe you got an idea. Fact is, every time we go by Fort Sam I get this idea, and I think you just decided me."

17

"What's that, boy?" his father asked.

"To join the Army. Right here at Fort Sam."

"But shucks, boy, you ain't but sixteen. You gotta be eighteen."

"Well I look like I'm eighteen. And who's gonna say different? You won't, will you, Pa?"

Monroe Dean scratched his head thoughtfully a moment. "Well I dunno. You kind of took me off base here, boy. If you go in the Army, and with Elmer gone for Lord knows how long it'll take that fool boy to catch up with us, that leaves just me and Paul here to work."

"That's the point of it, Pa," Jerome said. "The work ain't been so good lately anyhow, it'll be easier for just you and Paul to get hired on somewhere than the three of us. And I'll be gettin' paid in the Army and fed and everything. Maybe even get to learnin' some kind of trade."

His father was silent a moment, rubbing a callused hand along his jaw, squinting into the Army post as they chugged along the road by the wire fence. "Still looks to me like a jailhouse with a mighty big yard," he said, half to himself. Then, in his voice a note of acceptance, he said to his son, "You're a high-spirited boy, Jerome, full of funnin' and carryin' on, and I learned you myself to take guff from no man, but to have respect for who earns it. They preach a life of obeyin' orders no matter what, in the Army. You're gonna have your nose to the blackboard again, like you did back in schooolmaster Dennis' class. You think you can take it, boy?"

"Cain't be no worse'n pickin' cotton fourteen hours

18

a day, Pa," Jerome answered soberly. "Might be a sight better, too."

Mr. Dean nodded his head. "That's it then. You drive me and Paul on into San Antone, then you can hitch a ride back to the fort and enlist."

So it was, the next morning, that Jerome Herman Dean awoke to the sound of the bugler blowing reveille. Confounding the records once again, he enlisted at Fort Sam Houston as Jay Hanna Dean and, with his father vouching for him, said he was eighteen, had been born in Holdenville, Oklahoma, and had graduated from grammar school. In 1926 record keeping on both the civilian and Army levels was haphazard enough to get him by the recruiting office, which was eager to find new new young recruits.

Jerome was already half awake when the bugle sounded. It was five thirty in the morning, dawn was just a crimson suggestion on the horizon, but dawn-to-dusk labor was the only life he had ever known, and he accepted the early call without a second thought.

As he began to dress hurriedly for roll call, the thought did strike him, however, that he was indeed in strange surroundings. His had been a life of spaciousness and movement, of cotton-white fields and blue skies, silver mountain streams and dark green forests, of bumping over rutted country roads, the old Fords hissing steam from the radiators, with nothing in front of him but the whole country if he wanted to travel it. Now, he thought fleetingly, putting on his faded work fatigues, now his

19

world had narrowed suddenly to the few acres of the Army post, a world all khaki brown and green.

Jerome, or, as he was known in the Army, Jay, was not from the very first an outstanding soldier. The snap and polish and regimental air of the career Army man was too contrary to his basic nature: casual, independent, confident almost to the point of swagger. Moreover, he was just sixteen years old and in fact only semiliterate, never having learned much more writing than his name and more reading than the most elementary.

With this background it was small wonder that he was assigned to the most menial tasks. He was attached to the Third Wagon Company of the Quartermaster Corps and given the job of keeping the stables clean, the Quartermaster Corps then being largely horse-drawn. As a raw recruit, young, awkward, with a seemingly eternal grin no matter the circumstances, Jerome was subjected to even more than the usual amount of hazing accorded an Army rookie.

When not in actual training in the field he got every dirty job in camp, and the more he took it all in his stride, grinning and joking in his good-natured, ingenuous way, the more he goaded his superiors to greater efforts. This was fairly normal procedure in the peacetime Army of 1926, however. Barracks life was crude, demanding, often pitiless. The boredom, the routine and the discipline often brought out the worst in the men, many of whom were not of superior character. With no war to inspire patriotism and the need of men of quality, with no promise of learning skills and trades at good pay,

20

the Army too frequently became the haven for the shift-less, the discouraged, the neurotic.

So Private Jay Hanna Dean, serial number 6233400, was treated no better and not much worse than any other recruit. He swept the stables, scrubbed the horses, cleaned the latrines, peeled potatoes and lay exhausted on his bunk at night with the rest. But where his bar-racks mates groaned, he grinned through it all, until one night the recruit in the bunk next to his asked him how he took it all with a smile.

The man, a lanky Texan, swung his legs off the bed and sat upright facing Jerome. "Ah just cain't figure you none, kid," the Texan, an older fellow, said. "They been givin' you the hind leg of the steer since you got here, and all you do is lie there in your sack every night grin-nin' away like a love-sick mule."

Jerome cupped his hands behind his head and squinted down the bed at the toes of his heavy Army shoes. "See them big ol' shoes, Slim?" he addressed the lanky Texan. "Some fellers'd call 'em ugly clodhoppers, and maybe they are that, come to look at 'em close up. But they're the first by-God shoes I ever could call my own. Never wore shoes much at all, back home, and when I did they was hand-me-downs from brother Elmer, and me and little brother Paul'd take turns a-wearin' 'em."

The young recruit sat up on his bed then and faced the Texan, his face suddenly serious. "There weren't nothin' I wore that weren't wore before me by brother Elmer and maybe our Daddy too, and Paul'd get 'em when I was through, with a bit of mendin' here and

21

there. I picked cotton in the fields like a man before most kids my age could wipe their own nose, and as for eatin', there was times I ate so much sowbelly I'd grunt like a razorback every time I opened my mouth.

"You wonder how I can take this here Army life and come up grinnin'? Well I ain't sayin' it's all side meat and corn bread, but I'm livin' a dang sight better than I ever did in my whole life."

Six months of Army life did little to change Jerome's attitude, except that the routine bored him. He was known around the company area as somewhat of a "Sad Sack," a good-natured, hard-working but rather inept youngster whose dress khakis never seemed to fit quite right, sandy hair often as not spilling out from under his garrison cap, tie hanging limply from an unbuttoned collar. He was neither disliked nor particularly well regarded by his barracks mates and resignedly tolerated by his superiors. In effect, he was accepted by the Army community at Fort Sam Houston as another buck private "sweating out" his enlistment time.

Only on the rifle range did Jerome prove to be outstanding. With his Arkansas mountaineer background he took to the Army's Springfield rifle naturally. His first time out at the qualification range he won a sharpshooter badge, prompting his platoon sergeant to stare in wonder.

"Dean," the sergeant said, "sometimes you're so clumsy you can't hit the barracks floor with a mop. How come you're such a hot shot with a Springfield?"

Jerome grinned at him. "I only just learned how to

use a Army mop, Sarge, but I been shooting a rifle for meat since before I even had enough teeth to chew it. Shucks, shooting at a big ol' paper target at a hundred yards is easy as hittin' a barn with buckshot. You shoulda seen me knock squirrels out of a gum tree at two hundred yards when I wasn't more'n ten years old."

"I know," the sergeant said sarcastically, "and I'll bet you always got 'em right between the eyes, too."

"Did better'n that," Jerome replied seriously. "Never even touched a hair of 'em. My Daddy taught me how to wait till that squirrel crawls out on a limb, see, then you shoot the limb out behind him, he falls to the ground and the drop kills him. You don't spoil no meat at all that way, like you would with a bullet."

It was on the long hike back from the rifle range that the Army took on added dimension for Jerome. Coming through the gates from a new direction, into a part of the vast camp that he had never entered before, he saw a neatly laid out baseball field. Hurrying his pace to close up behind the corporal marching in front of him, he said, "You fellers play baseball in this here camp, or is it just for the officers?"

"The officers don't play, they watch," said the corporal. "We got regular teams in each company, a league, kind of, for the whole camp. Why? Don't tell me back in those Arkansas hills you even saw a baseball, Dean?"

"Well maybe not a real good one," Jerome said. "Most of the time we'd just have some fun, me and my brother Paul and my Daddy, chuckin' hickory nuts at one t'nother and hittin' at 'em with a hoe handle. But once

23

in a while when we was travelin' around during the cotton-pickin' time we'd get us a real game of baseball goin' with the other hands. My Daddy once made up a real good ball, twistin' lots of rubber bands around a golf ball then coverin' the whole thing with black tape. Lasted us two years, that ball, till somebody hit it into a crick. It was down near Shreveport. I remember it like it was yesterday. My Daddy was near fit to bawl, he worked so hard makin' that thing."

"So your Daddy taught you how to play baseball," the corporal said, his skepticism apparent in his voice. "Anything special you can do?"

"Well, I learned to pitch some."

"Tell you what, Dean, if you can pitch like you can shoot a Springfield, maybe we can use you. I'm on the team, play first base. We start practicing in a couple of weeks. Come on out and we'll see."

"Knock it off back there!" the sergeant's voice bellowed at them. "No more talkin'! Dean! Get back in ranks where you belong!"

Jerome fell back in his place, a new feeling of pleasure buoying him along as he continued the march. He turned his head for a long look back as they passed the ball field, then, snapping to attention as the sergeant called his men back to cadenced marching order, a satisfying thought crossed his mind.

"Maybe joinin' the Army wasn't such a durned fool idea after all," he said to himself.

3 ••••••

The baseball field at Fort Sam Houston, which was, in fact, a series of interlocking athletic fields used by the entire camp, came alive one Saturday morning of an early Texas spring. Uniforms of the several different fort teams mixed with the green fatigue clothes of the new men trying out, among them Jerome Herman Dean. He stood off to a side near one of the wood and chicken wire backstops, looking in awe at the display of professional-type equipment. Never at one time, and in one place, had he seen so many clean white baseballs and shiny bats —and the gloves, still smelling pleasantly of new leather.

After a while he found the corporal he had spoken to on the march and approached him confidently. "Here I am, Corp," he said, tapping him on the shoulder.

The corporal turned and looked at Jerome. "Well if it ain't Walter Johnson himself," he said. "Didn't really expect you to show you, Dean, but as long as you're here we'll give you a chance to show your stuff." He introduced the young private to some of the other team members, then brought him to a player wearing the equipment of a catcher, who was the team's playing manager.

25

"This here's Private Dean, Sarge, come all the way from Arkansas to pitch us to the post championship," he said, winking broadly.

"That so?" said the catcher, taking the corporal's cue. "Well we're mighty grateful to have you, Dean. Pitch a little professional ball down Arkansas way?"

"Shucks no, Sarge," Jerome said, unaware of the byplay between the two men, "I ain't hardly pitched in real baseball games at all. But I can throw real hard, and inshoots and outshoots and all, and I'd sure like to join up with your team."

"Inshoots and outshoots, eh?" the catcher repeated, smiling. "Okay, Dean, grab a ball and a glove and get out to the mound. I'll catch you and see what you got. And see if one of the boys has a pair of spikes you can borrow instead of them big boots you got on."

"Spikes?" Jerome said, sitting on the ground and beginning to remove his Army shoes. "I ain't never wore 'em. I'll just throw the way I'm used to, if'n you don't mind." He rose then, barefoot, and taking a ball and glove from the corporal strode out to the pitcher's mound.

The sight of the barefoot youngster heading for the middle of the diamond stopped the practice session for most of the men, who turned to see what was going on. A few of them shouted wisecracks at Jerome, who ignored them and continued on his way. At the mound he scuffed his feet around in the dirt, examining with his toes and the soles of his feet the texture of the ground and the raised mound itself. Then he faced toward home plate.

26

"I'm gonna throw a few easy ones first," he called to the catcher. "I ain't never pitched off'n a real pitcher's mound like this before, an' I wanna kind of get used to it."

The catcher nodded and went into a semicrouch as Jerome curled himself into a big windup and threw his first pitch. It popped loud and hard into the catcher's mitt, right across the center of the plate. The catcher straightened and nodded and threw the ball back. Jerome squeezed it in his hand, feeling the newness, thrilled just to be standing on a real baseball diamond, throwing a professional-style baseball. He threw half a dozen more pitches, simple fast balls without all his speed behind them, then called to the catcher that he was ready to pitch in earnest.

"Watch it now, Sarge," he said. "I'm gonna throw real hard now, an' some of them inshoots and outshoots, too. You got one of them sponges you can put in your glove so's your hand won't get hurt?"

The catcher stared at him. "You kiddin' me, Dean? I once played pro ball in the minor leagues. Just throw. I'll catch anything you got."

"Sure Sarge, sure, I didn't mean no insult," Jerome said apologetically. "Let's go."

The catcher squatted into position. Jerome wound up and threw a fast ball that sped across the plate and exploded into the catcher's big mitt like a rifle shot. The sergeant said nothing, returning the ball, but a curious look was in his eye. Jerome threw several more fast balls, the sounds echoing across the diamond, now com-

27

pletely quiet as every player in sight watched the barefoot recruit pitch.

"How about a couple inshoots now?" Jerome called. "You ready?"

The catcher stood up, took his hand from the mitt and rubbed it along the side of his uniform pants. "Yeah, I'm ready," he said quietly, his face a study in surprise and respect.

After a dozen pitches the catcher called a halt and beckoned to one of the men on the field. "Hogan, you get in here and catch a while. I want to get a bat and hit against this kid."

Jerome grinned. "Hey, that's great, Sarge. Should I let you hit some to the men in the outfield, or can I try to strike you out?"

"Yeah, try to strike me out," the catcher said dryly. "Let's see you do that."

In a moment they were all ready. Jerome wound up and threw a fast ball across the plate. The sergeant lunged and missed. The next pitch he fouled back. Jerome threw again, calling out, "Here comes an inshoot, Sarge!" The catcher, a right-handed hitter, set himself as the pitch came in over the outside corner. He swung evenly, but the ball broke down and away from him; he missed it by a full two inches.

Some of the watching men broke into laughter and jeers, and the sergeant's face turned red. Realizing his embarrassment, and embarrassed himself for the man, Jerome eased up on the next pitch. The sergeant hit it on a line to deepest left field. "Haw!" Jerome cried, "you sure hit me good that time, Sarge!"

But the sergeant wasn't fooled. He smiled thinly. "Okay, Dean, I guess you showed me enough." He walked to the mound and shook the youngster's hand. "I don't know where you learned it, hiding up in the Ozarks all these years, but you can sure throw a baseball."

Jerome grinned widely. "I tol' you I could."

The sergeant nodded. "All right, we'll get you a uniform and a set of spikes. Consider yourself on the team."

Jerome frowned. "Do I have to wear them spikes? I don't know as I can throw wearin' them things."

"Yeah, you gotta wear 'em. That's the rules. Besides, first game you got into some guy'd cut your feet to ribbons on the bases."

Jerome sighed. "I guess maybe you're right. Sure'll feel funny, though," he said, looking down at his bare feet. "Hard enough to wear shoes all day without wearin' 'em when I'm funnin'."

Word spread quickly around the post about the barefoot pitching character from the Third Wagon Company, and soon the team's practice sessions acquired an audience, including a number of officers. Many observers came to jeer at the young pitcher, though he no longer pitched barefoot, but even the most skeptical went away muttering about Jerome's booming fast ball and sweeping curves. Nothing like them had been seen before in the memory of the oldest veteran of the fort.

By the time the informal season opened at Fort Sam

Houston, everybody was waiting to see how good the kid pitcher would be in actual competition. There were many who believed that despite the speed and skill he showed in practice, actual competition against some of the post's good teams would rattle his confidence.

"Wait till he faces some of those good hitters from the artillery teams," one man said. "Then we'll see if he's really got anything or is just a hotshot practice pitcher."

The doubtful ones had not long to wait. The Third Wagon Company's first game would be against the formidable team from the Twelfth Field Artillery, and Jerome was scheduled to pitch. His own teammates, too, were anxious to find out just how good he was.

The captain of the Twelfth Field Artillery team was a tough top sergeant named Johnny Brought. Aside from his service stripes and his ribbons, Johnny Brought's pride was vested in the championship his baseball teams won annually in Army competition. Using his powers of persuasion and the influence of his stripes and years of service, the sergeant managed each year to assemble the best service team not only at Fort Sam Houston, but in the entire southern and southwest Army service areas. Somehow he obtained transfers of personnel and changes in station, one eye always to the good of the Army, but the other on the soldier's throwing arm or batting power.

So it was again, in that summer of 1927, that Top Sergeant Brought opened the season at Fort Sam Houston confident of another trophy. He had heard from the Quartermasters about the cocky young private and his blazing fast ball. But he had a good pitching staff of his own and a collection of sluggers that often were too much for the professional pitchers they sometimes faced in exhibition games.

As Brought watched Jerome strut to the mound to pitch the first inning, he felt he had little to be concerned about.

"Let's knock that Arkansas hillbilly out of there in the first inning," he told his men on the bench, loud enough for Jerome to hear.

The leadoff man stepped into the batter's box, a wide grin splitting his face. On the mound Jerome curled into a big windup and let go with a fast ball waist high over the inside corner.

"Strike one!" the umpire called.

The Artillery man backed out of the box, stepped back in again, the grin still on his face, but now doubt in his eyes. Another fast ball flew from Jerome's right hand. The batter swung and missed as the ball boomed into the catcher's mitt.

Backing out again, the Artillery man scooped up a handful of dirt and rubbed it between his palms. When he stepped back in, the grin was gone from his face. He looked out at the mound, his eyes curious and respectful.

Jerome looked toward the plate for the sign from his catcher, who was using a basic system of one finger for a fast ball, two for a curve. At that point anything more complicated was considered too much of a burden for the young pitcher to learn. Two fingers were showing now; Jerome threw a sweeping curve that broke down and

31

in on the fists of the left-hand batter. The man swung and missed for strike three.

A cheer went up from the Wagon Company ranks, but the catcher hurried out to the mound. "Waste one when you get two fast strikes," he said. "Make the guy bite for a bad one, keep 'em guessing."

"You mean throw a ball when I can throw a strike?" Jerome asked, acting surprised.

"Yeah, throw a ball. And don't act like you never heard of it before. I only tol' you a hundred times already."

"Okay, Sarge, if'n that's what you want me to do. Only it just don't make no sense at all."

"Don't worry about making sense. Just do what I tell you."

Jerome shrugged as the catcher turned away and went back behind the plate. To the next batter he threw three straight curves, all for balls, then two more curves for strikes. On the three-two pitch he threw a fast ball that whistled past the hitter's flailing bat—another strikeout!

Grinning, Jerome waved to the catcher. "I wasted three of 'em that time, Sarge," he called out. "Did I do good?"

The catcher grew red as a beet under his mask. "That crazy kid's gonna give me a heart attack yet," he muttered to himself.

The third hitter was Johnny Brought himself. He stepped into the batter's box warily, staring intently out at the mound. "This hillbilly as good as he's looked so far?" he asked the catcher. "Or are my guys just not warmed up yet?"

"He's just a wild kid," the catcher said, very much

32

aware of Brought's ability to steal good players. "Fast, but wild. If he goes more'n a couple innings I'll be surprised."

Brought grunted, crouched, cocked his bat as Jerome began his windup. A fast ball blazed by him for a strike. Brought swung at a curve, fouling it back for strike two. Then Jerome threw two curves that missed. A fast ball was fouled back. Brought swung at the next pitch, a curve, and dribbled the ball to the second baseman, who threw him out easily.

"Fast but wild, eh?" Brought said as he passed by the catcher, who was backing up the play at first. "Who you kidding?"

For four innings Jerome and the Artillery team pitcher matched each other, hurling scoreless ball. Wagon Company had gotten two hits, Jerome had given up just one, a pop fly single that fell in front of the center fielder's lunging grab. Artillery failed to get a hit again in their half of the fifth, bringing up Jerome himself to lead off the second half of the inning.

He let the first pitch go by for a strike, the next for a ball. He swung at the next pitch, a fast ball, and sent it rocketing out toward left field. It sailed high over the fielder's head, dropping to the ground and rolling free, with no fence to stop it. By the time the left fielder caught up with the ball, Jerome was around second and headed for third. He kept right on going around the bag as the long throw came in toward the infield, scoring standing up for a home run.

He jogged to the bench, shaking hands with his teammates. "Easy as hittin' hickory nuts with a hoe handle," he said to them.

That turned out to be the only run the weak-hitting Wagon Company scored. But it was enough. Jerome allowed just two more hits, a double and a single, the rest of the way, for a 1–0 victory. He struck out Top Sergeant Johnny Brought twice, and ten Artillery men in all.

At the end of the game, as he was being congratulated by his teammates and friends of the Third Wagon Company, he was called aside by Brought.

"Dean," the sergeant said, "how'd you like to become an Artillery man?"

Jerome thought of the countless days he had spent cleaning out the Quartermaster stables. "They got horses in the Artillery, Sarge?"

Top Sergeant Brought smiled. "Not for a guy who can throw a baseball like you they don't."

Jerome grinned back at him. "Then I'd like it fine, Sarge. Jest fine."

4 ••••••

While Top Sergeant Brought began his campaign to have Jerome transferred to the Artillery, the young pitcher continued winning games for the Third Wagon Company—between his regular Army duties, of course. Baseball had only a limited effect on his stable-cleaning chores, for while his newly displayed talent popularized him among his barracks buddies, it made little impression on the officers of his unit. To them Dean was still a well-meaning but rather inept soldier.

The significance of this attitude was not lost on Jerome, however. That summer, when he received his first visit from his father and brother Paul, he outlined his idea to them.

"There's one officer in particular in this here outfit thinks I ain't fit for naught but hawg callin'," he said. "Which suits me fine."

"Yankee, I betcha," his father said.

"Talks like one," said Jerome. "Anyways, he's always givin' me the terriblest things to do, an' all I do is smile away at him all day long. Makes 'im madder'n a flea hound with a busted paw. I figger if'n I can keep him mad at me it'll make it easy for that Sergeant Brought to git me a transfer."

"Haw!" burst out Paul. "If'n only Elmer was here now to hear ya tell it. You turned out right clever in the Army, brother."

"Oh I learned a few things," Jerome said pridefully. "But say, Pa, ain't you heard nothin' at all from Elmer?"

"Nope. Heard about him though, couple or three times. Folks down Chickalah way said he passed through just a few months ago. Headin' for Biloxi, said he was, though I cain't figger why. Nothin' much to do around Biloxi 'cept fish. We ain't worried, though, Paul and me. We been makin' out fine, and someday we'll ketch up with Elmer. Tell him all about how good you're doin' in the Army."

There was no game or practice scheduled that day, so Jerome could not show off his talents. He did, however, show his father and brother the ball field and the equipment, and he glowed with pride at their awe of the professional display.

"You done a good thing, enlistin' in the Army," his father said as they said good-bye at the gate. "By the time your hitch is up I betcha you'll be as fat as a brood sow and have money in the bank to boot."

Paul hugged him and shook his hand. "If'n I didn't have to help Pa I'd enlist in the Army, too," he said. "I been doin' some fair baseball pitchin' myself on Sundays, ain't I, Pa?"

"So ya have, Paul, but the Army ain't jes' playin' base-

36

ball. Main thing is you gotta be a good soldier, and you ain't cut out for soldierin' like your brother is."

"Pa's right, Paul. I'm a lot bigger for my age than you are. You stay and help him. When I get out we'll all get together again, and we'll find Elmer too, and we'll get us maybe a nice little farm someplace. Right?"

"Right," said Paul.

"You're talkin' like a man now, Jay Hanna," said his father. He and Paul climbed back into their old jalopy and drove away. Jerome watched them for a few moments, then he set his lips firmly and returned to his barracks.

Texas baked under an unrelenting sun; a drought settled over the land. The cattle lowed mournfully and their flanks grew thin. The crops wilted and browned. But Jerome Herman Dean flourished. He grew taller and broader, his fast ball whistled, and his curve ball dipped away from the bats of the hitters. He did not lose a game for the Third Wagon Company, pitching three shutouts, winning five games.

Toward the end of August he was summoned from his stable chores and told to report to the company orderly room. He hurried along the walk and up the three steps, pushed open the screen door and marched briskly to the desk of the top sergeant. The man looked up, silently thumbed him into the office of the company commander.

"Dean," the officer said when Jerome had entered and saluted, "sometimes the Army works in wondrous ways. Maybe I should have had more interest in your pitching baseball than in your pitching hay. You seem to be better at it. Anyway, for some strange reason, at which I need hardly guess, orders have come through transferring you to Battery A, Twelfth Field Artillery. The orders also say you've been promoted to private first class. Congratulations."

Jerome's face split into a broad grin. "Hot dawg! I mean, yes Sir! Thank you, Sir! Private first class! Wait till Pa hears about this!"

The company commander barely suppressed a smile. He found it difficult to dislike the young soldier despite his seeming indifference to Army discipline. He stood up and extended his hand. "Good luck, Dean," he said. "I'd consider it a personal favor if you wouldn't request a transfer back to Third Wagon Company."

Jerome burst out laughing, noting the smile on the officer's face. He shook the man's hand vigorously. "Ain't much chance of that, Sir. I seen enough of stables and horses to last me the rest of my born days."

Jerome picked up his orders and his promotion from the sergeant, returned to his barracks to pack his things and walked the distance to the Twelfth Field Artillery section at the other end of Fort Sam Houston.

The Twelfth Field Artillery won the post championship again, aided substantially by their new pitcher, who turned around and beat his old mates from the Wagon Company in the final and deciding game of the season. Jerome lived well all that fall and winter, coddled and protected by Top Sergeant Johnny Brought, who foresaw perennial pennants flying from the Twelfth's head-quarters flagpole.

But the 1928 season was not that easy. A year older in terms of age and Army service, Jerome had grown wise to the ways of the world. Word had leaked out to the semiprofessional teams of nearby San Antonio that a young fast-balling phenomenon lived at Fort Sam Houston. On pass in town early in the spring of 1928, Jerome was asked by one of the teams to pitch for them when he could get into town. He would be paid, of course.

It was perfectly legal, within Army regulations, and Jerome jumped at the chance to earn extra money. The one drawback was Sergeant Brought. "The Sarge'd never let me pitch in between games for the outfit," he told one of his friends. "He'd be afraid I'd pitch my arm sore."

"Well it's true. You won't be able to pitch so good for him if you pitch for them civilian teams in between times," the soldier replied.

"Shucks, I could pitch every day in the week and it wouldn't bother me none," Jerome boasted.

"So then don't say nothin' to Brought. What he don't know don't hurt him."

"Good idea,' said Jerome. "An' so's he'll never catch on I'll pitch extra good for the outfit on Sundays."

The scheme would have worked fine, for in truth it did seem that Jerome had an iron pitching arm, but for the fact that Brought came into San Antonio one day to see a ball game and found his star pitching. With a roar of rage he leaped onto the field and pulled Jerome off the mound.

"You crazy hillbilly!" he shrieked. "The whole outfit's depending on you to win the pennant, and you come here to throw your arm out for a few extra bucks!"

"But Sarge," Jerome replied calmly, "I been winnin' every game I pitched for you, ain't I? Nothin's fairer than that, is there?"

For the moment Brought was stumped by Jerome's logic and apparent innocence. Then he exploded again. "No, it ain't fair! Did I pull strings and stick my neck out for you and get you out of them stables with a PFC stripe just so you could pitch for a civilian team? Where's your loyalty to me?"

Jerome looked sullenly down at his shoe tops. "I didn't figger it that way, Sarge. I just thought, so long as I keep winnin' for the Twelfth it wouldn't matter if'n I picked up some extra money in town."

"Well it does matter. You can't keep on pitching here on Saturdays and winning for us on Sundays, I don't care how strong you are. Now you gotta cut this out, understand?"

Jerome sighed. "You're the boss, Sarge."

For two weeks Jerome obeyed orders. But the itch began again. Lying on his bunk one evening he confided his thoughts to a barracks mate. "I keep thinkin' of that farm me and Pa and the boys want to buy someday. Cain't save much money on my Army pay. I could use that extra money I was pickin' up playin' in town."

"Yeah, but you can't blame Brought either," the other man said. "He brought you here to pitch for us, not no

40

civvie team. You know you can't really pitch that much and be any good to us every week."

"But that's just it," Jerome insisted. "I know I can."

The soldier shrugged. "Don't convince me. Convince the Sarge."

Jerome knew it was useless to try swaying Sergeant Brought, so that Saturday morning he simply took his week-end pass and slipped quietly into San Antonio. He pitched, and won. The next day he pitched for the Twelfth, and won—but he was hit hard. Only the superior batting power of his teammates saved the day for him. Sergeant Brought said nothing, but his eyes narrowed as he watched Dean walk wearily off the mound after the game.

The following Friday, after evening chow in the mess hall, Jerome was picked up by two military policemen as he walked back to barracks. "What's up, fellas?" he asked, startled, when the MP's stopped him.

"Don't ask me, Dean," one of them said. "All I know is we got a pickup order on you. Gotta take you to the guardhouse."

Protesting and uncomprehending Jerome let himself be escorted to the guardhouse, where a sergeant locked him in a cell.

"Ain't a man got no rights!" he yelled. "What am I in here for? What'd I do?"

"Save your breath, Dean," the sergeant growled.

"I wanna see Sergeant Brought," Jerome demanded. "He'll get me outta here!"

41

The sergeant grinned at him. "It was Sergeant Brought who gave us the pickup order on you."

Jerome's jaw fell open. It hit him suddenly. "That sidewindin' rat!" he yelled, pounding on the bars. "That mis'able mule-eared rattlesnake! He stuck me in here so's I cain't get to town and pitch tomorra! That's it, ain't it, Sarge!"

"I don't know from nothin', Dean," the sergeant said. "All I do is pick 'em up and lock 'em up."

"But . . . but, he's gotta have some charge to keep me in here, don't he?"

"He'll find one that'll stick, don't worry about Johnny Brought."

"Then I won't pitch for him on Sunday. I'll show him," Jerome said. "He cain't make me pitch if I don't wanna."

"Well now, of course, I can't speak for the Top Sarge, but I got a hunch that if you don't pitch on Sunday, and win besides, you'll be right back here on Monday. In fact, you might move in here permanent like until you do pitch and win."

Jerome's eyes bugged. "You mean you can do that to me in the Army?"

"We're doin' it, ain't we? Now you just be a good boy and do what Johnny Brought says and you'll be all right."

Stunned, Jerome sat down on the rude bunk in his cell. He was too surprised by the sudden turn of events to be bitter, even angry. Besides, his general good nature usually kept him from feeling such emotions as anger or resentment. He remained quietly in the guardhouse until

Sunday morning, when Sergeant Brought came to fetch him to the ball game.

"Sarge, how could you do this to me?" he asked. "I never been so lonely in all my born days. No visitors, nobody to talk to, nothin'."

"Just call it a rap on the knuckles to teach you a lesson, just like you was in school," the sergeant said, smiling. "I want you in condition to pitch your best on Sundays, and if this is how I gotta keep you from pitching in town, then it's the way it's going to be."

"I learned my lesson, Sarge," Jerome said, but secretly he was thinking of ways to fool Brought again. Now it was not only a question of extra money, but a challenge to his ability to outwit Johnny Brought. "And just to show you there's no hard feelings," he continued, "I'm gonna pitch extra good today."

"Your usual will do," Brought said.

Jerome was as good as his word. That Sunday he completely confounded a team from the Medical Section, pitching a two-hit shutout, striking out eleven, batting in two runs himself in a 4–0 victory. After the game, as he was changing into fatigue clothes, Brought came over to him and shook his hand. "Beautiful game," he said. "And now I want to tell you something. I didn't want to tell you before because I didn't want to make you nervous. But it'll explain why I was so hard on you, throwing you in the guardhouse like that.

"You see, kid, there was a major league scout out there today. A scout from the St. Louis Cardinals. He came all the way down here just to see you pitch."

Jerome's jaw dropped. "From the Cardinals? To see me pitch? But how come, Sarge? Who tol' 'em about me?"

"I did. You see, kid, I'm what they call a bird dog for the Cardinals. Like a scout's scout. The regular scouts can't cover every inch of territory they're assigned, watching all the ball games, so they hire part-time guys like me, who know a little something about baseball talent, to kind of sniff out young kids like you that maybe got a chance to be pros. That's why they call us bird dogs."

"Sure, I understand about that part, Sarge. Had a bird dog back home myself, once. Name of Suds. But what'd you tell that feller that made him come down here to see me pitch? You don't really think I can be a professional baseball player, do you, Sarge?"

"I do. And don't play innocent with me, Dean. I know you like a book. I only *think* but you're *sure* you can pitch pro. Am I right?"

Jerome grinned. "Well, sometimes, like today, I do get the feelin' I got the callin'. Like some fellers do for preachin'."

Brought nodded. "So I told this scout—I told him you're the clumsiest kid I ever seen going into a windup, but you can throw hard and you got a good curve." Brought paused, then he added, "I also told him you were the dizziest kid I ever had in my outfit."

Still grinning broadly, Jerome said, "Me? Dizzy?"

"Yeah, you," Brought replied. "Dizzy."

5 ●●●●●●

In short order the story of the Cardinal scout's visit made the rounds of the fort, and with it Top Sergeant Johnny Brought's new nickname for Jerome. "Dizzy" Dean, the eccentric young right-hander from the Twelfth Field Artillery, he was known from then on. Happy with his new name and impressive status with the men on the post, he confided his feelings to Brought one afternoon. "I was a real nothin' and with no place to go afore I came here," he said. "Now lookit me. Every time I pitch I got all them captains and colonels out there watchin' me like I was somebody important. I tell you, Sarge, enlistin' in this here Army was the smartest thing I did in my whole life."

"And the smartest thing after that was beating my outfit when you was with the Quartermasters. If we had beat you, you'd still be scrubbing horses and sweeping stables."

"But what do I do now, Sarge? Just wait? Is that scout still comin' around? Did he like the way I pitched?"

"Whoa! Slow down there, Dizzy," Brought said. "Yeah, that scout'll be around again. He liked what he saw plenty. But they take their time, those scouts. They ain't buyin' anything off one look. They'll have to see you pitch plenty before they commit themselves to recommending you."

"In that case," Jerome said, hesitantly, "wouldn't it be a good idea if I pitched in San Antone on Saturdays, and you was to tell him I was there, so's he could see me pitch more?"

"No, it wouldn't be a good idea!" Brought barked. "Am I gonna have to throw you in the guardhouse again or are you gonna be sensible for once!"

"Okay, okay," Jerome said. "Don't get sore, Sarge. I was just thinkin', that's all."

"When you start thinking you get dangerous. You just pitch, Dizzy, and leave the thinking to me."

The summer of 1928 passed swiftly with no word from the Cardinal scout. He returned several times to watch Dizzy pitch, and each time he saw a winning, impressive performance. Sergeant Brought, who knew the man well, could get no more than a "Looks promising" comment from him. Disappointed, having been confident that the Cardinals were ready to pluck him right out of the Army into the major leagues, Dizzy brooded all that fall and winter.

It was soon after New Year's Day of 1929 that the loudspeaker on the orderly room roof called for him to report to the company sergeant. He climbed the steps of the headquarters barracks and marched in. The sergeant looked up at him and pointed to a man in civilian clothes sitting in a chair nearby. "You got a visitor, Dean. Man says he'd like to talk to you."

Dizzy's heart quickened. Could this be a man from the Cardinals, at last? He walked over and the man stood up, introducing himself. "I'm from the San Antonio Public Service Company," he said, and smiled at the crestfallen look on Dizzy's face. "Can we talk somewhere, privately?"

Dizzy shrugged, looking at the man curiously. "My barracks should be empty. Come on over there." He turned to the sergeant. "Okay if we go on over and talk in the barracks, Sarge?"

"Sure, go ahead. Just don't give him any military secrets."

"Shucks, Sarge, I wouldn't do that. Anyways, I don't even know any," Dizzy said.

The sergeant looked at him sharply, sensing that he was being kidded, but Dizzy's face was blankly innocent. Sighing, the sergeant waved him out of the office.

In his barracks Dizzy motioned his visitor to sit on the bed while he himself straddled a foot locker and leaned forward, resting his elbows on the iron railing at the foot of the bed. "Now then, what can I do fer you, mister?" he asked.

"Well, to come right to the point, you can come to work for us this spring." Then, pleased by the apparent puzzlement he was causing his young listener, he continued. "I don't mean to be so mysterious, Dean—Dizzy I hear they call you—but I'm playing a little game with you because I'll bet you two-to-one you thought I was a scout for the St. Louis Cardinals coming by to sign you up."

"You're a winner," Dizzy admitted, grinning. "But how come you know so much about me, and what's this here idea you have about me coming to work for you?"

"It's like this," the man said. "Our company has a baseball team, like a lot of companies all around the country have. It means a lot to the men who run the company that the team is a good one. It's for the men's morale, and it's good publicity for the company. So part of my job is to go around Texas looking for good young ballplayers to sign up for the company. Just like a major league scout, except for San Antonio Public Service."

"Well it makes a little sense," Dizzy said, " 'cept for a coupla things. First, what I do for your company when I ain't playin' ball, or is that all I have to do? Second, ain't you forgettin' I'm in the Army and my hitch ain't up yet? An' third, why would I wanna get out of a pretty nice life I got here to go to work for you? All I gotta do is keep pitchin' good ball here maybe another year or two the most and I'll get signed up by a major league club for sure. Johnny Brought says so."

"I know your Johnny Brought," the visitor said. "And I've got a lot of respect for him. But I think he's wrong this time. Let me tell you something, Dean. You'll never be picked up by a major league team here, because they don't think Army competition is worth a hoot in a blizzard. But the so-called company-team circuit is just one step below the regular minor leagues, and in some cases actually a step higher. The majors figure it that way, not me. And if you pitch good ball for us, then you got a good chance of getting picked up."

Dizzy frowned in thought. "You wouldn't be foolin' me about all that, would ya mister? I'm just a Arkansas boy what never had no shoes till about a year ago, and I gotta take a feller at his word 'cause I don't know much. Is what you say the truth?"

"It's the truth." The man smiled. "And you can forget that hillbilly act with me, Dean. I talked to a lot of people about you. They may call you Dizzy, but you're a lot smarter than you put on."

Dizzy grinned, flattered. "That so?" Then the grin faded. "But how about that other thing? My Army hitch?"

"There's a new Army regulation, came out about a year ago, you probably never heard of. It allows a man in peacetime to buy his discharge before his hitch is up."

"Buy his discharge?"

"That's right. How long you been in, Dean?"

"Since November of twenty-six."

"That's a little over two years in the service. All you got to do is pay the Army a hundred dollars, and you can get out any time you want."

Dizzy stared at him. "Well wouldn't that frost your eyebrows!" he exclaimed. "I'd never a knowed if'n you hadn't told me."

"Oh it was probably posted around long enough and printed in the camp newspaper," the man said. "You just never noticed it."

"No, I guess I missed it," Dizzy said, reluctant to admit to the man that he still could barely read.

"Well, that takes care of that problem. Now, as for

your job when you're not playing ball, it's an easy one. You read gas meters for us."

"Gas meters?" In his sparse existence before the Army, he had seen few homes with gas piped in. Most people he knew used kerosene to heat, light and cook with.

His ignorance was not lost on the man from the public service company, however. "Don't worry about it," his visitor assured him. "It's a cinch, and we'll train you." The man rose from the bed. "Well, what do you say, Dean? We got a deal?"

"I cain't rightly say," Dizzy said. "It all sounds right fine, but I think I oughtta talk with Johnny Brought and my Daddy afore I do anything."

"Good enough. But I'm rounding up this year's team right now. You got to let me know one way or the other in a week or so." He shook Dizzy's hand then and left.

Dizzy sat on his bunk for a long time after his conversation with the man from the public service company. The idea of leaving the Army for a job that included lots of baseball appealed to him greatly. Except for the baseball end of it, he had never fully adjusted to the routine and discipline of Army life, and the Army had never quite become accustomed to him. It would be no hardship on either, Dizzy knew, if he left the service. His only tie at all to the military life was his loyalty to Top Sergeant Johnny Brought. What would Johnny say about his quitting for a civilian job and a civilian baseball team?

That question uppermost in his mind, Dizzy roamed the company area until he found the sergeant overseeing a howitzer battery operation. When the exercise was over he took Brought aside and asked to talk to him. "How about a beer in the canteen?" he asked. "It's important, Sarge."

"Not now, Dizzy," Brought said impatiently. "I got a battery to train. How about tonight, after chow?"

That evening, in a corner of the canteen that afforded them some privacy, Dizzy told Sergeant Brought of the public service man's visit. "What do you think I should do, Sarge?" he asked.

"Do? There's only one thing you *can* do," Brought said. "That guy makes sense. I know that public service team. They're good. They've had guys picked up by the scouts before. I think you should grab the chance."

"But how about you, and . . . and the Twelfth?" Dizzy said, surprised at Brought's easy acceptance of his leaving the outfit. "Don't you want me to stay? I mean you're always tellin' me about how I should be loyal and all that stuff."

"Sure, sure," Brought said. "I know I said all that. And I meant it when I said it. I'd like you to stay with the outfit, Dizzy, but I'm not gonna stand in the way of your making it to the pros just to pitch for some two-bit Army post team."

"Two-bit! The Twelfth ain't no two-bit team! How can you talk that way about it, Sarge!"

"Now c'mon, Dizzy, cool off. You know what I mean. I know, I make a big fuss about the team. I pull strings and make deals to keep it the best on the post. Okay, I enjoy it. But it's still an Army post team, and you'd be

51

crazy to stay here. You can carry loyalty just so far, and then it becomes just plain stupid."

"Well, if'n that's the way you feel, Sarge, I guess I oughtta take that guy up on his offer, right?"

"Right. Talk to your Pa first if you want, but I think it's the smart thing to do. By the way, you got the hundred bucks you need to buy your way out?"

Dizzy shuffled his feet and looked at the ground. "No, I ain't. Afraid I spent just about all of my Army pay. But I got a few dollars and Pa must have a few. 'Tween us I reckon we'll make it okay."

"Well if you need any let me know," Brought said gruffly. "Maybe I'll loan you some."

Dizzy grinned at him. "Sarge, you're all right. Always knew you was. You might have been born in the Ozarks y'self you're such a right feller."

"Scram, go to sleep," Brought growled at him, embarrassed at his own display of generosity. "You got a hike ahead of you tomorrow on a battery problem."

With the enthusiastic help of his father, they scraped together their meager savings, borrowed from their few friends, including Sergeant Brought, and purchased Dizzy's discharge from the Army. On March 15, 1929, he walked through the gates of Fort Sam Houston a civilian again.

With a good, steady job now, he was able to keep the family together. They took rooms in a boardinghouse in San Antonio, hoping, by staying in one place, to come upon brother Elmer all the sooner. Only his absence prevented the Deans from being supremely content.

With the San Antonio Public Service Company Dizzy resumed the ways he had left behind in the Army. The company found him to be an extremely likable but less than enthusiastic worker, and an extraordinary pitcher. This, as in the Army, more than made up for his other deficiencies. Soon, as the company's recruiter had promised, the major league scouts began to drop by the company games as word spread about the new pitcher. Although it was a first look for most of the scouts, the man from the St. Louis Cardinals came with the experience of having watched Dizzy pitch an entire season at Fort Sam Houston.

Thus while the other scouts watched and wondered, the man from the Cardinals was able to make a decisive move. Toward the end of the summer of 1929, he came by the Deans' boardinghouse and offered the young pitcher a contract with the St. Louis organization. Considering what he was bringing, he expected some form of jubilation and expression of gratitude from the family.

Jubilation he encountered. The Deans whooped and hollered and danced around the kitchen table. But grateful though he might have been at heart, Dizzy was far too confident a young man to express gratitude. Instead, he clapped the scout on the shoulder and said to him, "Well shucks, man, what took you so long to make up your mind?"

53

6 ••••••

St. Joseph, Missouri, was a quiet town with a baseball team that represented them decently in the Western League. Occasionally there was a flurry of excitement among the true baseball buffs in town when a promising young player went on to better things in the major leagues, or on the rare occasions when the "parent" St. Louis Cardinals passed through for an exhibition game. But before or after the summer of 1930, its citizens were to remark for many years afterward, St. Joseph never experienced the excitement generated by the presence of Jerome Herman "Dizzy" Dean.

St. Joseph was where the Cardinals sent him for his baptism of professional baseball fire. It was considered a fair enough test, neither too easy nor too tough a league for his estimated talents. He arrived in town one spring day brimming over with confidence and a contract in his pocket for two hundred and fifty dollars a month. It was more money than he had ever heard of in his life. The money, and the heady knowledge that he was a professional baseball player, drove him wild. The restrictions of Army life that had served to constrain him were off now. He bloomed into a full-grown "character."

He marched into the St. Joseph locker room for the first time as though he had been born into professional baseball. There was none of the rookie reserve about him. He walked boldly into the manager's office, introduced himself and asked for his locker.

"It don't have to be a real good one," he said. "I don't figger I'm gonna be here the whole season anyways."

"No?" the manager said dryly. "Where do you expect to be going?"

Dizzy winked at him. "I know how it is. It wouldn't look right for all the other fellers if'n the Cards' manager, what's his name—"

"Gabby Street."

"Yeah, that's it. If'n Mr. Street sent for me right away them other fellers might think it ain't right, me bein' so young an' all. But when he sees how good I am up here he'll be sendin' for me right along, I bet."

The St. Joseph manager looked at him curiously. He couldn't believe this nineteen-year-old rookie, without a day of professional experience, could be serious. On the other hand, he didn't seem to be joking. Strangely enough, he said it all so openly that the manager found himself unable to resent his remarks. It was just too unbelievable.

"Tell you what, Dean," he said when he recovered from Dizzy's outburst, "I'll give you a locker right near the door, so when Street calls you, you can get out quick."

He sat back then and waited for his irony to penetrate. But he didn't know his man.

"Say, that's real nice of you, goin' to all that trouble for me," Dizzy replied.

"Don't mention it." The St. Joseph pilot scratched the back of his head in wonderment. This rookie, he thought, was either too dumb or too smart to be kidded. He suspected it was the latter case.

"One thing, Dean. I told the desk clerk at the hotel to phone me when you got in. How come he didn't? You did go to the hotel first like you were instructed in the letter that came with your train ticket, didn't you?"

Dizzy made a face. "I did go there. But I don't feel too comfortable in hotels, tell you the truth. I got me a room in a nice little boardinghouse just a couple blocks away."

"You got you a room, eh? Well you can just unget you a room. The players on this club live and eat in the same place, understand? I can't go looking for you all over town every time I need you."

"Shucks, you won't have to go lookin' for me," Dizzy said. "I'll be right there for breakfast every mornin' and at the ball park every day."

The manager sighed. "We'll argue about it some other time," he said. "Get into a suit and on the field. We'll see if you can pitch as good as you talk."

Dizzy did a lot of both in St. Joseph, adding some bits of clownishness that endeared him to the local fans, if not to his manager. Spotting a bicycle under the stands one day, he remarked to a teammate that he had always wanted a bike and promptly climbed aboard, riding it onto the field and out to the mound, where he signaled the batboy to come take it away. A bike became his trademark after that in St. Joseph. He rode one along the side lines between innings, "To keep in shape," he said. Sometimes, when the team was at home, he disdained the bus ride to the field and rode the bike, waving to people in the streets.

He spent money recklessly and was always broke, asking the club for advances on his salary. He ignored curfew regularly, staying out late entertaining. But he did it all so guilelessly, with such obvious good will for everybody, that his manager found it difficult to curb him.

He would have been fired or at least suspended, of course, were it not for the fact that none of these activities affected his performances on the ball field. No matter what else he did, Dizzy won ball games, and in brilliant style. He pitched, hit and ran the bases superbly, more than once winning a game singlehandedly.

In one such game, early in the season, he had a 3–0 lead in the sixth inning when he suddenly lost his touch. A single, a walk and a home run, and the score was tied. Dizzy walked a few feet off the mound and called to his manager. "Say, I'm right sorry about that. But don't worry, it won't happen again. I'll make up for it myself."

The fans sitting near the dugout burst out laughing; it wasn't the first time he had stopped in the middle of a game to call out an apology for allowing a hit or a run.

Ignoring the laughter, however, he settled down and struck out the next two batters to end the inning.

The score remained 3–3 through the seventh and

eighth innings. In the last half of the ninth, with two out, it was Dizzy's turn to bat. With nobody on base the manager let him hit for himself, saving a pinch hitter for a more promising situation.

Confidently, Dizzy dug into the batter's box. He let a ball go by, fouled off the next pitch, then hit a long drive that dropped into right center field and rolled all the way to the wall. Churning around the basepaths he slid headlong into third with a triple.

He stood up and dusted himself off. "I woulda hit a homer," he said to the third baseman, "but I figgered it would look better if'n one of the reg'lar hitters knocked in the winning run. I sure hope he don't disappoint me none."

The leadoff batter for St. Joseph hit the first pitch for a single, and Dizzy pranced across home plate for a 4–3 victory.

"I'll win twenty-five games easy," he boasted later to a reporter from the local newspaper, " 'cept I don't think I'll be here that long."

As usual, and to the consternation of those who resented his boasting, Dizzy was right. He didn't remain in St. Joseph long enough to win twenty-five games. By August he had a 17–8 record and was promoted to the Cardinals' Houston farm team, the Buffs of the Texas League.

The move brought the long-lost Elmer Dean back into the fold.

It had been almost four years since that long freight train had separated the family. Now, in August of 1930, sitting at a soda fountain in a Dallas drug store, Elmer saw a strangely familiar face looking at him out of the sports pages of the daily newspaper. Though he could barely read the story of how Dizzy Dean had won a ball game for the Houston Buffs the day before, the photo did look like his brother.

Elmer beckoned to the counter man, a friend of his. "This here picture look like my kid brother Jay Hanna," he said. "What does it say? Did he give up cotton pickin' to play ball?"

"It don't say nothin' about Jay Hanna," the counter man said. "They call him Dizzy Dean. He won a game yesterday for Houston. That your brother?"

"Must be," replied Elmer. "That picture sure does favor him, though we never called him 'Dizzy.' Ain't seen him nor the rest of family like to near four years. Could you maybe write a letter for me to Jay Hanna and send it to him in Houston? I'll give you my address and maybe he can come and fetch me. Sure would be nice to get together with Pa and my brothers again."

The letter was sent. Three days later Dizzy, Paul and Monroe Dean, roaring down dusty back roads in a big open touring car, rescued brother Elmer from the farm where he had been working.

"Ain't never gonna be separated no more!" Dizzy shouted on the way back to Houston. "I'm on my way to the big leagues, brother Elmer! There's gonna be plenty of money for all of us, and when I'm up there and important enough I'm gonna get them Cardinals to take on Paul, too. He ain't had his chances yet, but he can pitch

59

as good as I can—almost, anyways."

Elmer could scarcely believe his ears and eyes. The car, though not new, was big and clean and shiny. His father and brothers wore new clothes and looked prosperous. Traveling along with Dizzy as they did, they were able to get fairly good jobs with the help of the clubs he played for. For once in their lives money was not hard to come by. Though the stock market crash of 1929 had plunged the country into a general depression, the Deans, conversely, were emerging from a lifetime of depression into comparative plenty.

In Houston Dizzy continued his spectacular ways, on and off the field. Here, however, the fans and the team manager took him more in stride. The year before they had experienced a season of excitement with an eccentric young third baseman named Pepper Martin, who had since left for Rochester. A fiery personality who played hard on the field and sang hillbilly songs in the dugout as he strummed a banjo, Martin had set the stage for Dizzy's arrival late in 1930.

"Another lunatic," was the simple comment of the Houston sports writers soon after Dizzy arrived. Yet, like Martin, Dizzy had them pounding their typewriters in praise of him before long. He won eight games, lost two and struck out ninety-five batters in the eighty-five innings he pitched.

The Cardinals were impressed with their farm hand. Branch Rickey, the St. Louis general manager, had been following Dizzy's career from the beginning. The young pitcher's background and personality appealed to him.

Rickey was a strange man for the baseball world. He was an idealist, religious, evangelistic, a learned man who walked around the Cardinals' dressing room quoting the Bible. He never went to the ball park on Sundays. Characters like Dizzy intrigued him; he felt paternal toward them, tried to reform them.

By late September the Cardinals had the 1930 pennant secured. Rickey could afford to indulge his curiosity. He phoned field manager Gabby Street and told him to send for Dizzy. "Let the boy pitch one game," Rickey said. "Let's see what he can do."

7 ●●●●●●

The clubhouse of a major league pennant winner has a certain air about it that is readily apparent to most rookies fresh up from the minor leagues. The atmosphere is one of quiet professionalism. The clubhouse appointments—lockers, showers, etc.—denote class and care. The difference between a major league clubhouse and that of even a high minor league club is a wide one. Few rookies can walk for the first time into a major league clubhouse without a feeling of awe, as though they had entered hallowed ground.

But to Dizzy Dean the Cardinals' clubhouse might just as well have been Houston's, or St. Joseph's, or for that matter the barracks of the Twelfth Field Artillery. And the players, pennant winners though they might be, could well have been his old buddies from the Army. He marched in that September afternoon in 1930, expansive and grinning, clapping the men on the back, introducing himself and asking the players' names.

They were famous ones in 1930—Frankie Frisch, Jim Wilson, Burleigh Grimes, Chuck Hafey, Charley Gelbert, Ray Blades, Gus Mancuso and Wild Bill Hallahan. One and all they stared at Dizzy in amazement as he made himself at home, hung his street clothes in a locker, received a uniform from the clubhouse man and barged into manager Gabby Street's office.

"You'd think the busher won the pennant for us or something," second base star Frankie Frisch remarked to pitcher Grimes.

In Street's office Dizzy heaved himself into a chair and grinned broadly. "Well, here I am, Mr. Street," he said. "I told them in St. Joe when the season started there weren't no use in my unpacking all my stuff, and sure enough here I am."

Street had heard enough about Dizzy to be prepared, but he was still taken aback by the young man's brash confidence. Finally he recovered enough to answer him. "Well if I were you I still wouldn't bother to unpack," he said. "You're only up here because we already won the pennant, and Mr. Rickey thinks you deserve a treat for the way you pitched in the minors. Now maybe I'll let you pitch for a few innings today against the Pirates, but don't let it go to your head. It don't mean anything and I don't expect anything."

"Shucks, Mr. Street, you don't have to worry none about me. I'll beat them Pirates easy. Say, the way I feel today, bein' up here with the Cardinals, I'll bet them Pirates won't even see the fog on my fast ball."

Street closed his eyes for a moment, as though the action could shut out the image of the fresh bush leaguer sitting there grinning before him. But when he opened them again Dizzy was still there, grinning.

63

"All right, Dean. I can see now why they call you 'Dizzy.' If you can't pitch the other team dizzy you can talk 'em dizzy. I'll let you start today's game. Don't try to strike everybody out. Just try a few innings so we can get a look at you."

"A few innings? Why I'll pitch the whole game for you. You don't even have to keep anybody in the bullpen. Give the boys a rest. Shucks, you won the pennant anyhow; let them take it easy today."

"Just go out and pitch!" Street rasped at him. "Get back in the clubhouse and go over the signals with Mancuso. If you're going good maybe I'll let you stay in there. We'll see."

After Dizzy left the office the exasperated manager said to himself, "I hope the Pirates beat your brains in. Do you some good."

The Pirates found Dizzy as difficult as all his other opponents had found him: his fast ball jumped, his curve dipped maddeningly, and in Houston he had developed a tantalizing change-of-pace pitch that complemented perfectly his fast ball. Pitching effortlessly, as though the Pirates were not his first major league test but just another bunch of amateurs or minor leaguers, Dizzy won his debut, 3–1. He allowed the Pirates just three hits and struck out five.

"A fluke!" manager Gabby Street said afterward, but grudging admiration edged his voice.

As for Dizzy, he sang loudly in the shower and exchanged banter with his locker-room mates. Toweling himself a few moments later he called out to pitcher Bur-

leigh Grimes, "Make room on the bench for ol' Diz next
year, Grimes. I'm gonna see to it personally that the
Cards win another pennant!"

Some of the players laughed. But such boasting did
little to endear Dizzy to the men, or to manager Street.

Despite his irritating qualities, Dizzy was invited to
train with the Cardinals in Bradenton, Florida, in the
spring of 1931. Basically, ballplayers were not expected
to be paragons of brotherhood and good manners, just
good ballplayers. There seemed to be ample evidence
that Dizzy Dean was a prime pitching prospect. "If he
pitches even half as good as he says he does," Wild Bill
Hallahan remarked, "he'll be the best right-hander in the
league before long."

Dizzy arrived in Florida broke and full of plans. To
get out of debt he had made a deal with an aviator to
parachute out of the plane over the Cardinals' training
field, the event to be advertised in advance, tickets to be
sold and the proceeds split. "We'll do it on a Sunday,"
he told the pilot, "so's the folks can bring the kids and
we can sell more tickets."

The plot got as far as circulars being printed to adver-
tise the stunt. However, Dizzy told one of his teammates
about the idea, and the man wouldn't believe it until he
was shown the circular. Then he ran to manager Street
with the news. Street vetoed the idea quickly.

"You wanna get yourself killed, do it in the off-season
and not around the training camp," he said. "I got some
kind of responsibility for you, though Heaven knows

what I ever did to deserve the likes of a nut like you."

"I was just tryin' to make some extra money," Dizzy said, looking forlorn.

"You wanna make more money, pitch good enough to stay with the Cardinals this year," the manager said. "And try keeping your mouth shut at the same time."

"Pitch good enough for the Cardinals?" Dizzy repeated. "Why shucks, I thought I showed you last year I could do that. I'll win the pennant for you, you'll see."

Bad enough as it was that he bragged continuously to manager Street, Dizzy made matters worse by boasting to the reporters covering the Cardinals. Always eager for colorful copy and interesting interviews, the sports writers found Dizzy a delight. He was always ready to talk about anything, but especially himself.

"I'll win thirty-five games for the Cardinals," he said one day in spring training. "Well, be conservative and say twenty-five, and I'll surely not let you down. And hit? Say, I ought to hit three hundred against these cluck pitchers easy. I'm one of the best young hitters in base-ball."

Anxious to please the sports writers, flattered by their attention, Dizzy made up stories about his early life that he knew would intrigue them. To each reporter who interviewed him, however, he gave slightly different versions of the same story, resulting in a confusion in the newspapers about his personal life.

The angry reporters finally caught on to his act and demanded to know why he had been fooling them.

"Well gosh, fellas," he answered in all innocence, "I

didn't see much sense in telling you all the same thing. This way I figgered you each got what you could call an exclusive story."

So the spring of 1931 went. Dizzy drove everybody around him to a frenzy. "He's like a regular radio loud-speaker," commented one weary sports writer. "Trouble is you can't turn this guy off."

During exhibition games he sat on the bench, mur-muring to himself but loud enough for manager Street to hear, "I jest wish I was pitchin'. I'd get them guys out easy." In his loud but friendly manner, he offered advice to the veteran Cardinals on how to pitch, hit, throw and run. What exasperated the players even more than the constant stream of advice was the fact that more often than not it was good, sound advice.

During an exhibition game against the Philadelphia Athletics one day, Dizzy was grumbling as usual on the bench, this time at the pitching of Wild Bill Hallahan. The Cardinal left-hander loaded the bases in the third inning with nobody out.

"I jest wish I was in there," Dizzy mumbled.

Manager Street had had enough. "Dean! Get in there and pitch!" he called.

Dizzy looked at him. "Me? Pitch?"

"Yeah, you. You're so good you shouldn't even need a warm-up. Go ahead. Let's see what you can do against these guys."

Dizzy jumped up with a grin and ran out to the mound to replace Hallahan. As he took a few warm-up pitches, manager Street mused that this time the young pitcher would surely learn his lesson. These Athletics would not be the soft touch the Pirates had been the season before. Champions of the American League two times in a row, they had a fearsome line-up of sluggers. Now, with the bases loaded, their three top men were coming up to face Dizzy.

First man to step in was Al Simmons, the left fielder and two-time batting king of the American League. Dizzy struck him out on three straight fast falls. As Simmons walked away from the plate, shaking his head in wonderment, first baseman Jimmy Foxx stepped in—Foxx, next to Babe Ruth, was the best home run hitter in baseball.

Dizzy missed with his first pitch, a low curve. Then another curve was good for a called strike. Foxx swung at a fast ball and missed. Dizzy looked down for the sign from his catcher, shook off the curve sign, nodded at the fast ball, then called out to Foxx, "Hey, here comes another one of them foggy ones. Let's see you try and hit it."

Foxx believed him and dug in, waiting for the fast ball. Dizzy wound up and gave him one, letter high over the inside corner. Foxx grunted with the effort of his swing—but missed for strike three!

The exhibition crowd roared. On the Cardinal bench, manager Street shifted nervously. This wasn't what he had expected.

Now came Mickey Cochrane, the best catcher in the league and a dangerous hitter.

"Let's see you fog 'em past me, busher!" he challenged Dizzy.

Dean grinned down at him. "Three fast ones, comin' right up!" he yelled back.

He wound up slowly, kicked his left foot high and came down overhand with a fast ball. Cochrane swung and missed. Another fast ball. Again Cochrane missed. He stepped out of the batter's box, scooped dirt on his hands, stepped back in again, his eyes narrowly surveying the fast-balling right-hander on the mound. He found what was happening to him difficult to believe. Again Dizzy threw a fast ball over the plate and again Cochrane swung and missed. Strike three!

Dizzy had struck out in order three of the American League's best batsmen.

Street let him finish the game, and he beat the Athletics, 6–2. He was sure now that the Cardinals would keep him for the 1931 season, but Street ordered him sent back to Houston. He called Dizzy into his office one day in late April and told him why.

"You probably could win twenty-five games for me," he said, "but you'd ruin the ball club. Right now you've got the rest of the guys on the team chewing nails and fighting among themselves, they're so mad. About one more week of listening to you pop off about how great you are and they'd of strangled you sure."

"But I—" Dizzy began.

"No buts!" Street barked. "You got to get it through your head that you're strictly a bush leaguer on a team that was good enough to win the pennant last year. You may be great, but nobody wants to hear it. We didn't need you last year to win the pennant, and we won't need you this year. We'll win the pennant without you, whether you think so or not. So *adios,* kid. Maybe I'll see you next year."

Sadly Dizzy packed his bags and took the train for Houston, but by the time he arrived his spirits had risen again. "Shucks," he told himself, "trouble is those old-timers like Street don't understand a feller like me. I'll jest have to pitch so good in Houston this year that them St. Louis fans'll demand they bring me back."

The train pulled into Houston on a Sunday at noon. Dizzy picked up his bags and headed first for a phone booth. He called the ball park and asked for the manager of the team the Buffs were playing that day.

"Say, this is Dizzy Dean," he announced when the manager picked up the phone. "I'm back in town and, brother, I can hear you gnashin' your teeth right now. Jest thought I'd call you and let you know I'm pitchin' against your team this afternoon. I'll give them two, maybe three hits."

He gave them two. He also hit a home run to drive in Houston's only two runs.

There was one compensatory item for Dizzy in his return to Houston in 1931. It enabled him to see again Patricia Nash, a salesgirl in a Houston department store he had met the year before. Dizzy had fallen in love at once with the pert young lady, wooing her in typical Dizzy style, loud and bragging. Being a sensible girl, Pat understood him. She let the braggadocio slide by and saw underneath it the big gangling country boy with a generous heart and an eagerness to be everybody's friend.

From St. Louis at the end of 1930, from Dallas where he had made his home in the winter and from Florida in the spring of 1931, Dizzy had scribbled her a few lines. Now he was back in Houston and resumed his pursuit. He called her and called on her. He sent her expensive gifts and sang hillbilly songs to her late at night under her window.

Pat held him off until June. Then she consented to marry him.

"Yippee!" Dizzy shouted the evening she accepted his proposal. "Pat, darlin', we're goin' to have the bestest weddin' Houston's ever seen. I got it all planned. We're gonna get married this Sunday. Right at the ball park with all those thousands of people there a-watchin'. I'll buy hot dogs and soda pop for everybody. The preacher'll perform the ceremony right there at home plate. And for a weddin' present I'll pitch both ends of the double-header—and win both games, of course."

Pat laughed, her eyes sparkling with delight. "You're just plain loco," she said to him. "We're going to do no such thing. We're going to city hall and get a license and with just a few of our friends we're having a quiet ceremony. And the first thing I'm doing after we're married is stop that crazy way you spend money. Imagine! Buy a whole ball park full of people hot dogs and soda pop. No wonder you're not only broke but in debt up to those big ears of yours!"

Which is exactly what they did. And at city hall Dizzy had to borrow the two dollars for the license.

Pat did serve to settle him down, however. He realized,

71

first of all, that as a married man he had responsibilities. He kept better hours, let Pat handle his money and quieted down around the clubhouse, but not so much that anybody noticed the change right away. Pat talked to him, and some of her advice was finally beginning to come through.

On the field Dizzy was better than ever. He was the best hitting pitcher, the best fielding pitcher, the best base-running pitcher and in 1931 the best pitcher in the Texas League. He won twenty-six games for Houston, lost only ten, struck out three hundred and three batters, led the pitchers with a 1.53 earned average and set a league record with eleven shutouts.

He was named the Most Valuable Player in the Texas League, clinching the award with an amazing display of talent and strength in the final days of the season. With Houston battling for the league championship against the Fort Worth team, he beat them in both ends of a Sunday double-header to clinch a tie. Then, with but one day's rest, he came back to pitch and win again on the final day of the season, giving Houston the league title.

There was no holding him down now. Though the Cardinals had indeed won the pennant again without him, and the World Series too, their key players and pitchers were getting old. New blood would be needed, volatile, eager young men like Dizzy Dean.

Dizzy knew it. This time he refrained from his usual bragging—at least for himself. He hadn't forgotten a promise he had made nearly two years before. He informed the Cardinals in St. Louis that he had a brother

72

Paul wasting away on a farm in Dallas, a brother who could throw a ball even harder than he could. "Me and Paul will win all your pennants," Dizzy wrote.

Such generous praise from an egotist like Dizzy convinced the Cardinals of Paul's merit. When Dizzy got his orders to report to the Cardinals in 1932, Paul was signed by St. Louis and sent to the Columbus club for minor league experience.

Still Dizzy couldn't remain completely silent. He was bursting to brag to somebody about how the Cardinals had finally seen the error of their ways and brought him up for good. Finally he scrawled a note to a St. Louis reporter he had met the year before.

"I'll be seeing you soon," he wrote, "when the supposed great hitters of the National League get tired of trying to follow my fast one as it fades by them into the catcher's mitt.

"You know Dean," he concluded, "always good—even on an off day."

8 ••••••

Unhappily for Dizzy and the Cardinals of 1932, time caught up with them. Most of the players were veterans on the downhill side of their peak years. At twenty-one Dizzy was not only the youngest player on the club but one of the few under twenty-five. The fire and flash that had led them to two pennants in a row seemed to have gone, and manager Street couldn't get them going again. For the most part the trouble with the Cardinals was that they couldn't hit.

Dizzy complained about this bitterly. "These clunks are wastin' all my good pitchin'," he said to all who would listen early in the season. "It's gettin' so bad I may have to play the outfield in between pitchin' so's they can use me at bat. I'm hittin' better'n most of them so-called sluggers."

As usual there was enough of the truth in his vocal swagger to make it hurt in sensitive places. But nobody said a word to him. Bogged down as they were in the second division, the Cardinals knew they would have hit rock bottom were it not for Dizzy's pitching—and his all-around play.

74

There was a game early in May against the New York Giants, for example. Losing 1–0 in the last half of the seventh inning, Dizzy came to bat with orders to bunt. On the first pitch he squared away, but when third baseman Johnny Vergez dashed toward the plate, Dizzy shifted quickly and popped the ball over his head into short left field. With first baseman Bill Terry also in close for the expected bunt, second baseman Hughie Critz ran over to cover first while shortstop Travis Jackson headed for second base—all these movements taking place on the pitch as Dizzy squared away.

Now, however, the whole Giant infield had to shift into reverse, like a motion picture film suddenly flashing on the screen backward. Jackson had to back-pedal to left field to retrieve the ball, leaving second base uncovered. Dizzy, running alertly, took in the whole picture at a glance. He wheeled around first and headed for second, racing Critz for the bag. Jackson retrieved the ball and threw too late to Critz—but Dizzy never stopped. He wheeled around second and headed for third, again alertly noting that nobody was there! Jackson was still in left field while third baseman Vergez and young pitcher Hal Schumacher were near home plate, gazing dazedly at the mad spectacle of Dizzy running bases.

Vergez finally shook himself loose and charged toward third. Critz timed his throw to meet him but heaved the ball wildly past the base. Dizzy just kept on going, turned third and sped home with the tying run.

The play unnerved Schumacher and the Giants completely. Four more runs poured over the plate that inning before the Cardinals were retired. Dizzy meanwhile shut out the New Yorkers the rest of the way for an eventual 6–1 victory.

In the clubhouse later the Cardinals expected another Dizzy Dean outburst. Though probably the loudest and most flamboyant man in baseball, he had become, by comparison with the old Dizzy Dean, a subdued person.

All he said in the clubhouse was, "Say, if those Giants are the team we're supposed to beat for the pennant, the folks better start making their reservations for Sportsman's Park, St. Louis, right now. I'll say one thing, though. That Bill Terry is a good hitter. About the only feller in the league who makes me stop and think what I'm gonna throw."

"How about Jackson?" a sports writer asked. The Giants' shortstop was regarded as one of the better hitters in baseball.

"Jackson? A pipe," Dizzy scoffed. "I just throw my fast ball past him."

It was manager Street this time who sang the young pitcher's praises. "There's a great young pitcher who's learned something in the last year," he said to the reporters. "You may not think it to hear Dean broadcast about himself, but he's really about the smartest pitcher I ever saw. He's got the fastest ball in the league right now, and good control. And he's got instinct. One time is all he's got to pitch to a batter and he seems to sense the man's weakness. Not only that but he helps himself with his hitting and fielding. He's like a cat out there, a fifth infielder. He makes plays veteran pitchers aren't smart enough to think of."

"May be true," said one sports reporter, "but last year you had to farm him out because of his big mouth. You think he'll talk himself off the team again?"

Street shook his head. "Part of the kid's trouble is that he thinks he's always got to push to be recognized. I told him in spring training that he'll stick with the club no matter what he says. I think that helped. That and his getting married. Diz is a character, let's face it," Street concluded. "If he ever took himself and life seriously he'd probably become one of the great pitchers of all time. But then, he wouldn't be Dizzy Dean, would he?"

Dizzy continued to exist more or less quietly until early June, when he showed up late at the ball park one day and refused to get into uniform. "You won't let me pitch today no matter what," he said to Street. "Why should I bother putting on my uniform?"

Street looked at him curiously. "What's eatin' you all of a sudden? You've been behaving yourself up to now, why start trouble?"

" 'Cause I ain't bein' treated fair and square. I only get to pitch on Saturdays and Sundays so's I can draw big crowds, and that ain't enough, twice a week. I cain't win enough games that way, and next year when I ask for more money they'll say I didn't win enough games. How can I win if'n I don't pitch? It's hard enough winnin' anyways the way this team's hittin'."

"Listen, Diz," Street said, drawing a deep breath and letting it out in a loud sigh. "You're being treated okay.

77

Maybe you don't like your pitching rotation, but I'm the manager and it's got be the way I say. Now why don't you suit up like a good kid and we'll talk about it some more."

Reluctantly Dizzy obeyed. But a week later, in Philadelphia, he left the team suddenly and caught a train for St. Louis. "I'm gonna have it out with Mr. Breadon hisself," he said, referring to Sam Breadon, the Cardinals' president.

This time, he said, the problem was money. He was earning three thousand dollars a year under his Cardinal contract, and felt that because of his early season showing he deserved more. Breadon agreed to a small raise and a refund of an allowance to Dizzy's father that had been taken out of the pitcher's salary. Nevertheless he was warned that quitting the team that way would earn him next time, not a raise, but a suspension without pay.

Satisfied, but contrite, he sent his manager a telegram from St. Louis. "I'm sorry I left the club like I did, and if you will give me a chance to pitch in Philadelphia on Sunday and in New York again on Wednesday I will show you how games should be pitched."

Street let him have his way. He shut out the Phillies, but the Giants gave him more trouble. He was losing to them, 2–0, and muttering to himself once again about his lack of hitting support. Again he took matters into his own hands. Coming up in the fifth inning with two men on, he hit Giant pitching ace Carl Hubbell for a home run and a 3–2 lead. In the seventh he doubled another run home. The Cardinals finally won, 6–2.

There were too few such instances in 1932, however. The Cardinals just didn't have the power or the pitching depth. Though he led the National League that year in strikeouts, shutouts and number of innings pitched, Dizzy's won-lost record was a good, though not spectacular, eighteen wins and fifteen losses.

"With some hitting," manager Street lamented, "Diz could just as easily have been twenty-five and eight. And maybe we would have finished better than sixth."

It was difficult to tell by the final standings, but the 1933 Cardinals, though finishing fifth, had the makings of a dangerous ball club. For one thing, they were an angry team from the day in mid-July when Gabby Street was fired as manager and was replaced by Frankie Frisch. The players had expected Jimmy Wilson, the popular catcher, to inherit the job. Instead Wilson was let go soon after Street.

Called "The Dutchman" around the league, Frisch was a tough, stubborn, crusty veteran, one of the great second basemen of all time. Many of the Cardinals may not have liked him, but as a manager they respected and obeyed him. He lit a fire under the Cardinals soon after taking over the helm, but there just wasn't enough fuel to keep it burning long enough.

More than Frisch's personal drive, however, was the gradual jelling of the team as a whole that made it look so promising by the end of the 1933 season. Two gaps in the line-up were filled effectively with the addition of Joe "Ducky" Medwick in left field, and at shortstop a fiery ex-Yankee, ex-Cincinnati Red who once threatened to club Babe Ruth with a bat—Leo Durocher.

With just one more front-line hurler to follow behind Dizzy Dean, the Cardinals might have made a fight for the pennant. Dizzy repeatedly asked the St. Louis management to promote his brother from Columbus, but Paul's record did not warrant it. Dizzy carried the load virtually alone, doubling as a relief pitcher when asked, often making the suggestion himself when he sensed that Frisch was reluctant to use him too often.

Dizzy won twenty and lost eighteen in 1933, leading the league in strikeouts and completed games. And, on July 30, just a few days after Frisch took over the club, he pitched one of the greatest games of his brilliant career.

A huge crowd filled Sportsman's Park to capacity that Sunday to witness the double-header between the Cardinals and the Chicago Cubs, the 1932 National League champions. Opening the double-header against the Cubs' Guy Bush, Dizzy began badly. A double by Mark Koenig and a single by Babe Herman promptly scored a run. He retired the next three men, but when he returned to the bench Frisch warned him, "I'm taking you out next inning if you don't do better."

"You worry about gettin' two runs, that's all," Dizzy countered. "I just didn't warm up good."

The Cardinals got the run back for him in their half of the first, and it was 1–1 until the fourth, when two more Cub hits scored a second run. Dizzy bore down hard in the fifth, striking out the side. In the sixth he struck

out two more, and his teammates rewarded him with a
five-run rally, helped along by his own double in the
middle of it.

Leading 6–2 now he reared back and called for a little
extra speed. In the seventh he got Koenig on a pop fly,
struck out Babe Herman for the third time and retired
Kiki Cuyler on a pop-up to Martin.

Incredibly, he seemed to be getting faster every inning.
It appeared as though he had abandoned the curve ball
entirely, and in fact was just blazing the ball right over
the plate disdainfully, as though daring the Cub hitters
to even touch the ball.

In the eighth inning infielder Billy Herman looked
at three straight strikes, Frank Demaree fouled off one
pitch, then swung and missed at two more. Catcher Bill
Campbell hit nothing but air on three straight fast balls,
and again Dizzy had struck out the side. He was entirely
unaware of it then, and no one on the bench dared tell
him, that he now had a total of fourteen strikeouts, two
under the major league record.

In the Cardinals' half of the eighth inning, he belted
relief pitcher and ex-Cardinal Burleigh Grimes for a
two-run double, and went out to pitch the ninth inning
with a comfortable 8–2 lead.

"Maybe we should tell him how close he is to the
record," one of the Cardinals said to manager Frisch.
"With that lead he'll ease up and let 'em hit it."

"I don't think so," replied Frisch. "Diz is hot. I think
he'll keep fogging 'em through there. If we tell him he's
liable to press and blow the whole thing."

First baseman Harv Hendrick was the first man up. He inched his grip higher on the bat handle, trying to offset Dizzy's fantastic speed by whipping the bat around more quickly, but his effort was in vain. Three straight fast balls jumped past his flailing bat and he was strikeout victim number fifteen.

One more to go to tie the record, but Dizzy would have to strike out the side for the second straight inning to beat the mark. Four men in modern baseball history had struck out sixteen batters in a nine-inning game: Frank Hahn, Christy Mathewson, Rube Waddell and Nap Rucker. If he could at least tie these men he would be in august company indeed.

Dizzy was still unaware of his total. All he realized was that he had struck out plenty of Cubs, and that on the Chicago bench manager Charley Grimm was making faces and growling at him.

Dizzy forced himself to concentrate on the batter, shortstop Billy Jurges. He had struck him out once, and then twice, toying with him, had let him hit the ball; each time the shortstop had popped out. Now, however, momentum carried Dizzy through. Curling around in a big, exaggerated windup, he burned a fast ball past Jurges for a called strike. Another fast ball was swung at and missed.

One more strike to tie the all-time strikeout record.

Dizzy wasn't wasting pitches that afternoon. He blazed a third fast ball over the heart of the plate. Jurges swung and missed for Dizzy's sixteenth strikeout! He had tied the record!

The cheers from the Cardinal bench and from those in

the crowd who knew what he had done were lost on him; he figured simply that they were cheering because it was his fifth straight strikeout.

Pitcher Grimes was due to hit next, but Grimm was giving nothing away. He sent Joe Mosolf up to pinch-hit with orders to get at least a piece of the ball. "Anything but a strikeout," Grimm ordered, true to the baseball code. It was understood by all professional ballplayers that when a man is close to a record you make it as difficult as possible for him; only this way does a record-breaking performance have true value. No true sportsman, of course, would have wanted it otherwise.

Pinch-hitter Mosolf went up to the plate determined to hit the ball into fair territory at least, holding Dizzy to a tied record rather than letting him set a new one.

Dizzy reared back and threw the high hard one. The crowd roared. The Cardinals held their breath. Mosolf swung and missed! Again Dizzy threw the fast ball. Mosolf swung desperately but missed again.

One strike away now. The din in the stadium was deafening as word spread about Dizzy's nearness to the new record. He alone, it seemed, in the entire park, was unaware of where he stood, and the noise puzzled him. Ol' Diz really got 'em worked up, he thought to himself as he peered down for the sign from Wilson.

The catcher called for a curve, wanting his pitcher to waste one ball, figuring that in his eagerness Mosolf would bite at a bad pitch. Dizzy shook off the sign. Again Wilson hung it out and again Dizzy shook it off. Wilson

83

sighed behind his mask and called once more for the fast ball.

Everybody in Sportsman's Park knew the pitch would be a fast ball right down the middle. Mosolf set himself for the pitch, but before he could even swing, the ball had shot past him and exploded in Wilson's mitt for strike three!

Seventeen strikeouts! A new major league record for Dizzy!

He was halfway off the mound before that final pitch was even called, so confident had he been that Mosolf wouldn't touch it. The Cardinals leaped off the bench to meet him. His teammates on the field surrounded him and pummeled his back, until finally it was manager Frisch who told him he had set a new strikeout record.

"No wonder there was all that noise and ol' Charley Grimm hollerin' at me like that!" Dizzy exclaimed. "But I sure wish somebody'd told me earlier in the game that I had a chance for it. Shucks, I probably could of struck out twenty if'n I'da tried. I was just playin' around out there for a couple innings."

The victory, coupled with a 6–5 win in the second game of the double-header, jumped the Cardinals to third place over the Cubs. And in Columbus that same afternoon Paul Dean beat Toledo, 2–1. It was a day that augured well for the Cardinals' future, but nothing much came of it in 1933.

Manager Frankie Frisch was on a spot when the 1934 season began, and he knew it. His appointment had not been a popular one, he had barely improved the club's standing in his debut as its pilot, and the Cardinals, under the best of conditions, had a reputation for firing managers even when they won.

So when the team lost seven of its first eleven games, he barred the clubhouse to reporters one afternoon and laid down the law. "If you'd rather go back to the coal mines or the cotton fields or wherever you came from than ride around the country in Pullman cars and sleep in the best hotels, then speak up now. There's not gonna be no more room for softies on this club, get it? From now on it's no holds barred. That's the way we're gonna play ball!"

"Yeah," agreed Dizzy, "you said more'n a mouthful, Dutchman!"

By early May a new, rough-and-tumble bunch of Cardinals were in the thick of the battle for first place. At the Polo Grounds one day, in New York to play the Giants, some of the Cardinals were asked by a New York sports writer about their chances to win the pennant.

"We could win the pennant in any league," drawled Dizzy, "—the National or the American."

Shortstop Durocher shook his head. "They wouldn't even let a bunch of guys like us play in the American League. They'd say we were just a lot of gas house players."

And so the St. Louis Cardinals' immortal "Gas House Gang" was born.

9 ●●●●●●

There have been great teams in baseball and there have been colorful teams—teams like McGraw's Giants, Uncle Willie Robinson's Daffy Dodgers, Connie Mack's Athletics and Joe McCarthy's Yankees. But there never has been anything to compare with the Gas House Gang of 1934. There probably never will be.

In truth they looked and played like a bunch of toughs from the gasworks. Their trademark was a dirty uniform, and often as not they showed up at the ball park unshaven and unkempt. Their shins were cut and scarred from spike wounds received, and they retaliated in kind. As their manager Frankie Frisch had told them, it was no holds barred—and he couldn't have collected a more likely bunch of players to follow his lead.

There were Rip Collins at first base, Pepper Martin at third and, down the middle, two of the best umpire-baiters in the business, Frisch himself at second base and Leo "The Lip" Durocher at shortstop. Jack Rothrock was in right field, Ernie "Showboat" Orsatti played center and the black-tempered Joe "Ducky" Medwick covered left. "Spud" Davis and Bill DeLancey, another cracker-jack umpire-baiter, shared the catching chores.

Dizzy headed the pitching staff, and at last there was Paul beside him, brought up from Columbus. Behind them stood Dazzy Vance, Wild Bill Hallahan, Pop Haines and Tex Carleton.

It was a solid team, a talented team, made up of the last of baseball's rugged individualists. They fought each other, they fought the opposition, they fought the umpires and before the season was over even the commissioner of baseball. But always they fought to win.

After Frisch read them the riot act in May, they began to win. Where before they often would dissipate their energies in fruitless acts of anger, now they channeled their fierce drives against the other teams and fought hard when it counted the most.

But the Gas House Gang was not all blood and sweat. It was also, and perhaps most of all, laughter. Win or lose, angry or not, they were the most carefree, fun-loving, practical-joking aggregation in baseball history.

They dropped bags of water from hotel windows, and led by Dizzy and Pepper Martin, they sang hillbilly songs in the dugout. They wandered into staid ladies' luncheon meetings in the hotels and innocently sprayed the room with sneezing powder, claiming they were "exterminators."

In the middle of a terrible St. Louis heat wave they built a fire in front of the dugout, put on Indian feathers and wrapped themselves in blankets. In batting practice they carried each other piggyback in the outfield to catch

87

fungoes. Martin, a racing-car fancier, often drove midget racers right onto the field before a game and gave the howling fans a demonstration of his driving skill, circling the bases in the car while Frisch and the umpires chased him, threatening him with suspension for ruining the infield.

Once Martin showed up at a game covered with grease, wearing a mechanic's coveralls.

"Where have you been!" Frisch snapped. "It's almost game time!"

"I had a bet with a guy I could beat him a two-mile race. I had a little trouble with the engine but I beat him anyway."

"That's just great," Frisch said. "Don't I have enough to worry about without you racing those crazy midget cars? How much was the bet for, anyway?"

"A quart of ice cream," replied Martin calmly.

Dizzy carried his share of the joke burden. One day he carried a huge cake of ice onto the field and put it on home plate. "Got to cool off my fast one," he announced. "I feel real strong today."

Before a game in Boston he announced that he was taking no signals from his catcher. "Tell all the boys I'm throwin' nothin' but fast balls today," he said. He was as good as his word. He threw all fast balls, striking out ten men and pitching a three-hit shutout.

One of his most involved and most successful practical jokes worked so well in Philadelphia one evening that he and two other Gas Housers almost wound up in jail. At the Bellevue-Stratford Hotel, where the team was

88

quartered, a formal, dignified banquet was in progress. Dizzy peeked in, then hurried back to the lobby, where he rounded up Rip Collins and Pepper Martin. "They're all settin' around in there like a henhouse full of stuffed birds," he said. "I got an idea for some real funnin'."

A few moments later three men dressed in dirty overalls and painter's caps marched into the dining room dragging ladders and boxes of tools. Ignoring the diners the three "workmen"—Dizzy, Collins and Martin—set up the ladders, moved chairs around and began to work. While Dizzy hammered at the ceiling, Martin and Collins banged nails into the polished floor.

The toastmaster flew into a panic. He ran off the speaker's platform sputtering and stammering. "What—what's the meaning of all this?" he demanded.

From his perch atop one of the ladders Dizzy looked down at the bewildered man. "We don't know nothin', Pop," he said indignantly. "We jest got orders to start workin' in here."

The toastmaster fled but returned in a moment with the hotel manager, who recognized the Cardinal players instantly. He exploded in anger. "I'll have you put in jail for this, you lunatics!" he shouted.

But suddenly apprised of who the workmen were, the diners burst into laughter and persuaded the manager to relent. The Gas Housers happily paid for the damage caused by their hammering.

There were times, too, when Dizzy's jokes backfired. Against the Giants one afternoon he began easing up on player-manager Bill Terry because, as he had told his brother earlier, "That feller's in trouble. He thinks his team's gonna win the pennant. But we are. So I'm gonna let him hit a couple."

Terry began murdering the ball, with every hit slammed right through the pitcher's box. The first hit bounced off Dizzy's leg, the second ripped the glove off his hand. Still he eased up on his pitches, as the Cardinals led in the game, 8–1. When Terry's third straight drive almost hit him in the head, third baseman Pepper Martin trotted over to the mound. "If you don't mind, Diz," he said, "I'd like to give you a little advice on this guy."

"Yeah," said Dizzy, "what should I do?"

"Play him a little deeper," Martin said.

Another time, winning 7–0 in a game against the Cubs, Dizzy began lobbing the ball over the plate. Three straight Cub batters slammed the ball off the wall in left field, keeping Medwick on the run. After the third hit Ducky called time and strode deliberately to the mound. "Diz," he growled, "one more man this inning hits a ball my way and I rap a bat around your neck."

Dizzy started to make a joke, but he saw that his teammate was deadly serious. He gulped, nodded and struck out the next three men.

His ability to strike out men when he had to was hilariously demonstrated one day against Boston. Dizzy bet a friend, Johny Perkins, that he could strike out Vince DiMaggio four times. The bet was for a quarter on each at-bat.

After striking out Vince on three pitches the first three times, Dizzy decided to gamble everything. "Let's make it double or nothing on this last time—okay, Johnny?" Perkins agreed.

In the ninth inning, Dizzy threw a blazing strike past DiMaggio. Then another one. But on the next pitch the Boston outfielder caught a piece of the ball and lifted a high foul behind home plate. Rookie catcher Bruce Ogrodowski circled under it, waiting, when suddenly Dizzy came charging off the mound screaming, "Drop it! Drop it ya durn fool!"

Startled out of his wits the young catcher dropped the ball. Dizzy heaved a sigh of relief. He strode smiling back to the mound, wound up and threw a third strike past the waving bat of the frustrated DiMaggio. Dizzy had won his bet.

By early summer the National League pennant race settled down to a battle between the Giants and the Gas House Gang. "We'll win it easy," boasted Dizzy as he took time out to pitch in his first All-Star game. "Me and Paul will win fifty games ourself."

It was a fantastic forecast to make—for anyone else but Dizzy. By August they had won thirty games between them, and it did seem possible. Paul, a quieter version of his brother, was dubbed "Daffy" by the sports writers, and "Dizzy" and "Daffy" led the Cardinals through the hot summer in one of the closest pennant races in years.

On August 12 Dizzy and Daffy took a double setback from the Chicago Cubs, the first time all year they had both been beaten in a double-header. Dizzy's record then was 21–5, Paul's 12–6, but the double defeat threw them

91

into a temporary depression. Angry at themselves, they were ready for trouble.

It came in the clubhouse right after the second game. As the players were dressing, manager Frisch reminded them that the next day, instead of the scheduled off-day, they were due in Detroit to play an exhibition game. "So snap it up boys," Frisch said, "we only got about an hour to catch the train."

"I ain't goin'," Dizzy said suddenly.

"Me neither," said Daffy.

Frisch stared at them. "You two guys nuts?" he said. "Never mind, I know you're nuts, but what's the idea, you ain't goin'? What are you, privileged characters?"

Paul looked at his brother. "Diz," he said, "whyn't ya punch the Dutchman in the nose?"

Dizzy nodded. "I got a good mind to do just that, 'ceptin' he's smaller'n me. But we just ain't goin', me and Paul, and that's final."

"But for cryin' out loud why?" snarled Frisch.

" 'Cause Breadon and Rickey are two cheapskates, that's why, makin' us play exhibitions on our day off. Whyn't they pay us extra?"

Frisch sighed heavily. "I ain't gonna argue with you two screwballs. You don't want to go, okay, stay. But you're in for trouble, I can tell you that."

Two days later team president Sam Breadon fined Dizzy one hundred dollars and Paul fifty dollars for missing the game.

Enraged, Dizzy tore up his uniform. "We ain't payin'!" he yelled in the clubhouse.

"Hey Diz," a visiting newspaper photographer called, "I missed that shot of you tearing up your uniform. Could you do it again for me, please?"

"Why sure," Dizzy said. "Hey Paul," he called, "give me your'n so's I can rip it up for this here photographer." He proceeded calmly to tear his brother's uniform to shreds while the happy cameraman snapped away.

When the picture-taking was done, Dizzy resumed his protest. "We ain't gonna pay no fines, me and Paul."

"You'll pay," Frisch said. "They'll take it out of your salary, that's all. Now get out on that field and warm up."

"I'll go in a few minutes," Dizzy said sulkily. "I ain't ready yet."

Frisch suddenly lost his patience and his temper. "Never mind!" he snapped. "I'm suspending you, both of you, indefinitely!"

"Punch the Dutchman in the nose, Brother!" Paul cried.

"You cain't do this to us!" yelled Dizzy. "You wait. When the Cardinals find out how bad they need us they'll take back them fines! You won't win no pennant without us, Dutchman!"

"The heck I won't!" Frisch shouted back. "I'll pitch Hallahan, Haines, Walker, Vance and Carleton. And win, too!"

It looked like bravado on Frisch's part, since Dizzy and Daffy were his two best pitchers, but the Gas House Gang did win their next few games. On August 17 Paul surrendered and asked to be reinstated. He pitched the next day and won.

Dizzy was more stubborn. He was itching to pitch, but refused to give in without a fight. He contacted Baseball Commissioner Kenesaw Mountain Landis and asked for a hearing. Such were the days of the Gas House Gang that instead of Dizzy going to the commissioner's office, as would seem proper under the circumstances, the commissioner came to St. Louis to hold the hearing.

It was a noisy affair. Neither Dean brother was there, but many of the Cardinal executives, Frisch, the coaches and several players were present. Newspapermen were barred, but the transom over the office door was open and almost everything said was overheard and reported.

After reviewing all the evidence the commissioner decided that the Cardinals had been within their rights in suspending the Deans without pay. Further, they had the right to charge Dizzy for the torn uniforms.

"And one more thing gentlemen," Landis said, "as long as we're here. I understand that Dizzy has arranged to bring his brother Elmer to St. Louis so that he can sell peanuts at the ball park. I don't think it would look right."

"We agree, commissioner," said Breadon. "However, it's now settled. Mrs. Dean, that is, Dizzy's wife, also thought it would be improper and undignified. She vetoed the idea. Elmer won't be selling peanuts at Sportsman's Park."

The final decision cost Dizzy $486—$350 for seven-day's pay, the original $100 fine and $36 for the two uniforms he ruined.

Anxious to pitch again he accepted the decision—with

one complaint. "It weren't nice," he said, "makin' me pay for them uniforms. They coulda been mended."

Into September the pennant battle raged, the powerful Giants holding a five-game lead, the Cardinals barely holding second place over a tenacious Cub team. Now a new complication entered the Gas House Gang picture. Leo Durocher, their fiery shortstop, was in love. He wanted to marry Grace Dozier, a St. Louis dress designer, but she wanted to wait. Durocher's hitting and fielding began to suffer. He took his problem to Branch Rickey.

"I can't sleep thinking about her," he said. "But she's a Cardinal fan and thinks I should be worrying about the pennant instead of her. Meanwhile I can't play ball from all this worrying."

"I'll see what I can do," said Rickey, who knew the girl. He phoned her and pleaded with her to marry Durocher right away. "You're ruining a good shortstop," he said, "and our pennant chances with him."

"Now Branch," Grace said, "don't you think you're being a bit dramatic about this?"

"No, I don't think so," he said. "Now if you love this boy and call yourself a real Cardinal fan you'll marry him at once!"

That's how the Gas Housers acted that year, right to the top of the executive level. Grace was convinced by Rickey's argument, and a wedding date was set for the last week of the season. Durocher straightened out and played once more like a demon.

It was mid-September now. Time was running out for

the Cardinals—two weeks left in the season, and they trailed by five and a half games.

Into the Polo Grounds they came for a four-game series. The pennant could be lost in those four games; it couldn't be won, but with at least three wins, the Gas House Gang could put pressure on the Giants.

Paul Dean pitched the opener of the series and beat Freddie Fitzsimmons in a twelve-inning thriller, 2–0. But the next day the Giants won, 4–1. So far it had been a standoff—fine for the Giants, disastrous for the Cardinals. St. Louis had to take both ends of the next day's double-header or accept the inevitability of second place.

Dizzy was slated to pitch the first game against the Giants' great hurler, Carl Hubbell. More than fifty thousand fans jammed the ball park to see the two games that could decide the pennant that Sunday afternoon.

Both Hubbell and Dizzy were perfect for the first two innings. Then, in the third, Durocher singled with one out. Dizzy hit a hard ground ball to the Giants' shortstop that looked like a certain double play, but Durocher dumped second baseman Hughie Critz to break it up. With Dizzy on first Martin cracked a double to right center field. The relay from outfielder Mel Ott was a good one, but running like a wild bull Dizzy charged for the plate, slid in hard and knocked the ball from catcher Harry Danning's glove.

The 1–0 lead was quickly dissipated, however. In the New Yorkers' third, Ott homered with a man on base for a 2–1 lead. The Gas Housers came back with two runs in the fourth, the Giants one in the fifth. At the end of six innings the score stood 3–3, and the fans had screamed themselves hoarse.

In the seventh and eighth innings Hubbell and Dizzy were untouchable. Not a man on either team got a hit. Hubbell struck out four in those innings, Dizzy five. His fast ball was alive, jumping. He had abandoned his curve and change-up and simply threw the ball past the hitters.

As Rip Collins strode to the plate to lead off the ninth inning, Dizzy stood up in the dugout and called to him, "I'm up third this inning, Rip. Jest get on base and I'll send you home, boy!"

But Collins popped out. Durocher, however, walked on a three-two pitch. Dizzy stepped in, grinning widely. "You shouldn't oughtta have done that," he shouted to Hubbell. "I'm the best hitter on this here team, don't you know that?"

Hubbell smiled back grimly, stretched and broke off a curve ball. Dizzy let it slide by for a strike. Hubbell threw another curve and Dizzy slammed the pitch down the left field line. It hit the wall in one bounce and caromed off toward center field. By the time it was retrieved he was standing on second, and Durocher was back in the dug-out with the lead run. A moment later Martin singled, scoring Dizzy for a 5–3 lead. Hubbell struck out the next two Cardinals, but the damage had been done.

In the last of the ninth Dizzy swaggered out to the mound, struck out the first man on three pitches, got the next one on a pop fly to Durocher, and for the final out threw three blazing fast balls past Bill Terry for the ball game.

The victory was a tremendous morale booster to the Cardinals. They won the second game, also in dramatic fashion, when Pepper Martin broke up a tie in the eleventh inning with a two-run homer. The Cardinals now trailed by three and a half games, but momentum was on their side; pressure was mounting on the faltering Giants.

The New Yorkers were far from finished, however. They won three of their next four, while the Cardinals, rained out twice, won the two games they played. Then it was Friday, September 21. The Cardinals were in Brooklyn for a double-header with the Dodgers. Dizzy and Daffy were picked by Frisch for the two games.

Dizzy announced that morning to the reporters, "Zachary and Benge (the two Dodger pitchers) will go against no-hit Dean and one-hit Dean."

"Which is which?" a writer asked.

"Why I'm no-hit, of course!" said Dizzy.

The sports writers laughed, but not too derisively. Dizzy by now had a reputation for making his boasts come true.

For six innings of the first game it looked as though he had done it again. He retired eighteen men in a row. Then, in the seventh, he got the first two, but Ralph Boyle beat out a slow grounder to shortstop to break up the no-hitter. Dizzy gave up two more hits later, but won the game, 13–0.

It was brother Daffy who brought the prediction closer to reality. In the second game he pitched a near-perfect no-hitter. Except for a walk to Lon Koenecke in the first inning, not a Dodger reached base.

During the locker-room celebration Dizzy said, his arm around his brother, "Shucks, Paul, you shoulda told me you was gonna pitch a no-hitter, then I woulda pitched one, too!"

The victories were numbers twenty-seven for Dizzy, eighteen for Paul—forty-five victories between them out of a total of eighty-nine for the Gas House Gang, just over half.

Dizzy was pitching every other day now, an incredible pace. Frisch had told him, "You gotta do it for us, Diz. We can't afford to lose even one game, and you're the only guy I can depend on every time you go out there. You think you can do it, pitch every other game for us?"

"Dutchman, I'll pitch every day if you want me to," Dizzy said.

A rainout gave him an extra breather, but on September 25 he beat the Pirates, 3–2, for his twenty-eighth win. The Giants lost; their lead was now cut to one game.

The next morning Leo Durocher claimed his bride. That afternoon the Pirates' Waite Hoyt shut out the Cardinals. Fortunately the Giants also lost.

All that remained now was a final series for the Cardinals against the Reds while the Giants took on the Brooklyn Dodgers. Not only did the Giants have the pressure of a slump to fight, they had to contend with the wrath of the Dodgers. Before the season, Giant manager Bill Terry had been asked about the Dodgers' chances in the pennant race, and he had answered scornfully, "The Dodgers? Are they still in the league?"

The remark was to have its repercussions. The Dodgers lay in wait all year for the Giants. Now, with the pennant race at its climax, they showed Terry that they were very much in the league. They beat the Giants two straight while Dizzy blanked the Reds, 4–0, for his twenty-ninth win, and brother Daffy won his nineteenth, 6–1.

The Gas House Gang now led the league by one full game. With just one more game to go for each team, a tie was assured for the Cardinals. However, Frisch was taking no chances on a tie. He sent Dizzy against the Reds again, his third start in six days.

The St. Louis ball park was a madhouse even before that final game began. The crowd filled every seat and spilled over onto the stairways. They could smell a pennant in the making. Adding to the drama was Dizzy's bid for his thirtieth win plus the strikeout and shutout titles in the majors. But this was his ninth starting assignment in the last nineteen days, and he figured to be dead tired.

Could he do it? The crowd wondered.

Frisch was confident he could. "Dizzy's heart is as big as his mouth," the Cardinals' manager said before the game. "He'll come through."

The Dodger-Giant game in New York had already begun when Dizzy opened the game by striking out Sparky Adams. Joe Slade popped out, but Mark Koenig doubled. Frisch hurriedly waved to the bullpen to get started. The game was too crucial to depend on a tired pitcher. However, Dizzy got Jim Bottomley on a fly ball to Medwick, and the fans breathed easier.

The Reds' Si Johnson struck out Pepper Martin to start the Cardinals' turn, but then Rothrock and Frisch singled. After Medwick fouled out, Collins walked, filling the bases.

"Kayo" DeLancey stepped in then. "Just one run, that's all!" yelled Dizzy from the dugout. "One run and we win the pennant, Kayo!"

Kayo more than obliged. He drove Johnson's first pitch off the right field screen for a two-run double. Orsatti lined out, but Dizzy had a two-run lead.

With one eye on the scoreboard he settled down earnestly to pitch. For once his face was deadly serious. Not a smile showed, not a joke passed his lips. He reared back and fired his fast ball at the Reds, the pennant riding on every pitch.

They got a hit off him in the fourth, another in the fifth, but he kept them from scoring. Meanwhile the aroused Cardinals chased Johnson in the fourth with a three-run rally and scored once more in the fifth for a big 6–0 lead.

"They'll never beat ol' Diz now," a man in a box seat told his neighbor. "Nobody's scored six off him all year."

Three more times the Cardinals scored. Nine to nothing they led as the ninth inning began. Then, just as Dizzy took the mound, word was flashed from New York that the Giants and Dodgers were tied and were going into extra innings.

Dizzy wet his lips, and pitched to Jay Pool, who

101

promptly singled, the Reds' sixth hit of the game. Jake Schulmerich doubled and Adam Comorosky walked, filling the bases. The crowd was in an uproar. It had happened so quickly—Dizzy was tiring. Despite the scoring threat, the victory appeared certain. However, also riding on this inning was his seventh shutout of the season, which would make him the major league leader in that department.

At the mound now Frisch asked him if he was all right. "You done all you could, Diz," he said. "Nobody'd fault you if you was to come out now."

Dizzy started to answer when a sudden roar from the crowd made them glance up. From the outfield they could hear Orsatti and Rothrock yelling and pointing at the scoreboard. They looked. Numbers were going up showing the final score of the Giant-Dodger game. The Dodgers had won it in the tenth inning, 8–5. The pennant belonged to the Gas House Gang!

Jubilantly Dizzy grabbed Frisch around the waist and lifted him off the ground. "I'm gonna finish this one out myself," he said. "All of a sudden I feel like it was the first inning and I'm ararin' to go!"

Frisch grinned at him. "Go get 'em, Diz boy," he said, and returned to his position.

The crowd was chanting and stamping its feet now, rocking Sportsman's Park with the noise. They wanted to see Dizzy wrap up this victory in high style.

Catcher Clyde Manion was at the plate. The three Red runners inched off their bases. Dizzy didn't even bother to check them. He wound up and threw a strike past

102

Manion. He was grinning broadly now. A great weight had been lifted from his shoulders. The pennant was won. All he had to do was get the next three men without allowing a run for a dashing finale to an already spectacular season.

Manion swung and fouled the next pitch. The third one, a fast ball over the inside corner, he just gaped at as it sped by him for strike three. One out.

Ted Petoskey came up next, pinch-hitting for relief pitcher Allyn Stout. Dizzy struck him out, too, on three pitches. Two out. The crowd was near hysteria, overwhelmed at Dizzy's display of skill and courage, aware that he was putting everything he had into these final moments of the season.

Sparky Adams, the Reds' little second baseman, stepped in next. Dizzy gave him a fast ball over the middle. Adams swung and lifted a high foul near the Cardinal dugout. Everybody in the ball park held his breath as DeLancey circled under it. Would it be catchable—or in the stands out of play?

The ball came down right at the railing. DeLancey pressed against the fence, reached up and grabbed the ball for the third out and Dizzy's shutout. In the next second the entire ball park went wild.

Dizzy leaped off the mound, raced to DeLancey and tore the ball from him, racing for the dugout ahead of hundreds of fans who had climbed over the guard railings. They swarmed all over the field, ripping the clothes off the players' backs, grabbing their caps, leaping on one another in their excitement. Dizzy just did reach the

103

shelter of the dugout, a dozen fans at his heels. He ran full speed into the Cardinal clubhouse, clutching the precious ball in his fist, the ball that made him the shut-out king of the major leagues and the first man in seventeen years to win thirty games in the National League.

In a few minutes the Cardinals' dressing room was a shambles as the Gas House Gang celebrated.

"Me and Paul done it!" Dizzy shouted above the din. "Jest like I said. I said we'd win fifty games, and we won forty-nine. Woulda won fifty, too, if'n I hadn't lost a turn on accounta all that rain!"

It has been a delirious, fantastic finish to an altogether incredible season for Dizzy and the Gas House Gang. But there was more to come—a World Series with the Detroit Tigers that was to be one of the most exciting in baseball history.

10 ••••••

The stirring pennant drive of the Gas Housers was closely matched by the minor miracle of their American League rivals, the Tigers. Fifth the year before, they came back under the new leadership of catcher Mickey Cochrane to win Detroit's first pennant since 1909. "Black Mike," as Cochrane was called, had the great Hank Greenberg at first base, Charley Gehringer at second, Bill Rogell at shortstop and Marvin Owen at third. In the outfield, Joyner "Jo-Jo" White in center was flanked by Goose Goslin in left and Pete Fox in right.

The pitching staff was headed by the immortal Elwood "Schoolboy" Rowe, General Crowder, Elden Auker, Fred Marberry and Elon Hogsett.

The pattern of the series was set even before the first game began. A capacity crowd of more than forty thousand jammed the Tigers' Navin Field, watching the home team take batting practice, when the Gas House Gang trooped onto the field, still in their street clothes.

Resplendent in a sky blue topcoat and white sombrero, Dizzy strutted to the batting cage and took the bat from manager Cochrane's hands.

THE DIZZY DEAN STORY

"Let me show you how to hit, sucker," he said. The batting practice pitcher, furious, threw Dizzy a wicked curve. Dizzy promptly belted the pitch into the grandstand, calmly returned the bat to the apoplectic Cochrane.

He wasn't through yet. Walking over to the Detroit dugout, he poked in his head and said to Greenberg, "How come you're so white? You're a-shakin' like a leaf in a windstorm!" Grinning, Dizzy walked away before Greenberg could answer.

Cochrane passed up Rowe, his big winner, in the first game, risking Crowder against Dizzy. Or perhaps, as one observer remarked when the selection was announced, "Mickey's conceding the first game to Dizzy—that's why he's not wasting the Schoolboy."

In any case Crowder never had a chance. The Gas House Gang knocked him out of the box in five innings with four runs on two homers. When Marberry came in to pitch the sixth, Dizzy met him with a double. De-Lancey followed with another double. Martin, Medwick and Collins singled before Hogsett came in to quash the rally.

With his big lead Dizzy breezed along, the only big hit off him a homer by Greenberg. Final score of the first game: Cardinals 8, Tigers 3. But the best was yet to come.

Irrepressible Dizzy loved the limelight. He couldn't pitch every game of the World Series, but he could let everyone know he was there. When Frisch walked onto the field the following morning, he found his star pitcher sitting with the band, a tuba wrapped around his neck. Cheeks puffed and face red with effort, he was managing to emit an occasional brassy squawk from the instrument.

Frisch yelled at him to stop: "You lunkhead, you'll blow your brains out with that thing! Get on back to the dugout where you belong!"

"But shucks, Frank," Dizzy said, "I'm jest learning how to play this thing. Gimme another ten minutes and I'll play it good as this feller in the band."

Frisch had to threaten to carry him out bodily before he would leave, face pouting like a child's whose new toy had just been taken away.

Rowe tried to get the Tigers even in the second game, but fell behind early. A single by DeLancey and a triple by Orsatti got the Cardinals a run in the second. Singles by Medwick and Martin and a sacrifice fly by Rothrock made the score 2–0 in the third. The Tigers got one back in the fourth off Hallahan on doubles by Rogell and Fox, but the Cardinals went into the ninth leading, 2–1.

Fox opened for Detroit with a single. Rowe sacrificed. Pinch-hitter Gerald Walker popped a little foul along the first base line that either Collins or DeLancey could have had. But they let it drop between them. Given a second chance Walked singled in the tying run.

The tie held until the twelfth, when Detroit's "G men" broke it up. Gehringher walked. So did Greenberg. And Goslin singled to win the game and even the Series.

In St. Louis for the third game the crowd bought Dizzy Dean Hats—straw bonnets with red ribbons—and sat back to watch Daffy go against Tommy Bridges. Dizzy had sent a telegram to Branch Rickey before the game—collect, of course—advising him to relax. "I breezed through the first game with nothing on the ball but my glove," he said. "Tell everybody hello. Cook everyone a good meal, sandwiches and everything. We're coming home."

The Gas House Gang scored a run in the first inning on a triple by Martin and Rothrock's fly, another in the second when Paul's fly ball with the bases loaded scored Collins from third. Two more runs in the fifth gave Daffy a four-run lead, which he held to the ninth inning. A single by White and Greenberg's triple spoiled his shutout, but the Cardinals won, 4–1.

So far, except for the Gas Housers' pregame antics and the World Series atmosphere in Sportsman's Park, the games had been fairly normal. But, knowing the Gas House Gang, the fans and the sports writers waited for fireworks.

They began in the fourth game.

For good luck, that morning Pepper Martin ate a plate of apples, a ritual he had introduced successfully in the 1931 Series. Then Dizzy arrived at the ball park with a motorcycle police escort. He drove right onto the field and paraded around, standing up in a chauffeured convertible, police sirens screaming. The crowd loved it.

Martin's luck abandoned him completely, however. He made three errors. As for Dizzy, he sat on the bench, fretting as the Tigers blasted Tex Carleton for three runs in the third inning and reliever Dazzy Vance for one run in the fourth. The game was a close one then, though the Tigers led, 4–2. With Durocher on first, Frisch sent in Spud Davis to pinch-hit for Vance. Davis came through with a single, sending Durocher to second.

"Dizzy!" Frisch called. "Get in there and run for Davis."

"Run for Davis?" Dizzy echoed.

"Yeah, you know how slow he is. Besides, you're our good luck charm. I figure with you in there running bases we can get something going."

"Sure enough, Dutchman," Dizzy said. He rose from the bench and trotted to first base. A great roar came from the crowd as it recognized him. The fans felt the same way Frisch did; with Dizzy in there anything could happen.

Pepper Martin bounced to Gehringer, who flipped to Rogell at second for the force play. Rogell whirled and threw to first trying for the double play.

The ball hit Dizzy, running for second, right in the head. Down he went as though hit with an axe. The ball caromed off and bounced into right field. Running all the way Durocher scored the tying run.

The Gas Housers raced onto the field. Dizzy was out cold. They called for a stretcher and carried him into the clubhouse. While Doc Weaver, the Cardinal trainer, worked furiously over him, someone sent for an ambulance. Finally Dizzy opened his eyes. Painfully, he forced a grin.

"Well I guess I broke up *that* double play," he said. Then he lapsed once again into unconsciousness.

While an ambulance sped him to St. John's Hospital

the downcast Cardinals proceeded to kick away the game. Detroit won, 10–4. Once again the Series was tied.

At the hospital the doctors found nothing worse than a bad bump on Dizzy's head, but warned him against pitching too soon. Frisch was severely criticized in the St. Louis newspapers for risking his prize pitcher in a pinch-running role. With Dizzy out of the Series, the Cardinals didn't stand a chance.

Despite doctors' orders, he was there the next day, warming up before the game. "Ain't no bump on the head gonna keep ol' Diz outten the game," he said.

As Dizzy walked to the mound to pitch the first inning a fan leaped over the railing and ran to him, holding out a protective helmet. Dizzy laughed and put it on, then told the fan to leave it in the dugout for him. "I'll wear it when I get on base. I promise," he said.

It may have been, however, that Dizzy was not as well as he thought. He walked Greenberg in the second inning and gave up a double to Fox for one run. In the third the Tigers hit three straight line drives that, fortunately for Dizzy, went right at fielders. Then Goslin opened the fourth with a double and Rogell beat out a bunt.

With the dangerous Greenberg up next, Frisch trotted in from second and talked to his pitcher. "Whatta ya say, Diz? Maybe that ball conked you harder'n you thought? Maybe I should bring somebody in?"

"Scram, Dutchman!" Dizzy said. "Greenberg won't even get a smell of my fast one."

Frisch patted him encouragingly on the back and returned to his position.

110

Dizzy went to work on Detroit's famous slugger. He blazed a fast ball by him for a strike. A curve was outside for a ball. Greenberg swung and fouled the next pitch. Dizzy was beginning to feel the strain, though he grinned down at the batter. One more hit, he knew, and Frisch would have to take him out.

He stretched, looked over his shoulder at the runners, took a big step forward and poured a fast ball letter high over the inside corner of the plate. Greenberg swung and missed for strike three!

Still, it was only one out, runners on first and third. Up stepped Fox, who had driven in the Tigers' first run with a double. "Not again you won't," Dizzy said grimly to himself. He struck out Fox on three pitches.

Two out. One more to go. The runners led off their bases. Near second Frisch moved about restlessly, kicking at imaginary stones. No matter what else happened in the game he wanted Dizzy to get out of this jam. If Dizzy was knocked out of the box, the Cardinals' manager knew the morale of the whole team would be gone.

Marv Owen was up now. Dizzy curved him twice, then grooved a fast ball which Owen popped weakly to Durocher for the third out. The fans cheered. Frisch sighed in relief. Dizzy grinned at him as they climbed down the dugout steps. "Jest like I tol' you, Dutchman. I feel like I'm gettin' stronger every inning."

This time he was mistaken. While Tiger pitcher Tommy Bridges completely handcuffed the Cardinal hitters, Dizzy was touched for two more runs in the sixth, one on a home run by Gehringer, the other on an outfield error.

A home run by DeLancey in the seventh momentarily gave the Cardinals hope, but Bridges held them the rest of the way for a 3–1 victory. Dizzy had pitched a good game, giving up seven hits—but Bridges had pitched better.

The Tigers sensed ultimate victory with their triumph over Dizzy. They led in the Series, three games to two; they had beaten the Cardinals' best pitcher; and the final two games were to be held in their home park. To the experts, too, it appeared that the Tigers couldn't lose.

The Gas House Gang disagreed. "It's in the bag," Martin said on the train ride to Detroit. "Why sure," Dizzy sneered. "That Rowe ain't so hot. Paul'll beat him easy tomorra and then I'll win the last one."

Detroit was in a holiday mood that October Monday; Tiger partisans fully expected to proclaim their team World's Champions before the day was over. A record crowd was on hand to see Tiger ace Schoolboy Rowe beat another Dean—Paul this time.

But help came from a totally unexpected quarter— Leo Durocher, known in the league as the "All-American out." Though he fielded with his usual brilliancy in the Series, and was as noisy and aggressive as ever, he had lived up to his reputation by getting only two hits in eighteen times at bat for a .110 average. Frisch had even considered benching him in the sixth game for a stronger hitter, but no utility man was available who could ap-

112

proach him in fielding. So Frisch let him stay—and Durocher came through.

The score was 1–1 in the fifth when Leo began the inning with a single. Paul sacrificed him to second. When Martin followed with a single, Durocher raced around to the plate, taking out the catcher with a vicious slide. The relay from Goslin flew all the way to the backstop allowing Martin to scamper around to third. When Rothrock bounced a slow grounder to second, Pepper charged home with the third run.

Paul wasn't out of trouble yet, however. On their home grounds the Tigers were doubly dangerous. In the last of the sixth inning White led off with a walk. Cochrane singled him to third. Gehringer tapped back to the box, but Paul fumbled the ball, allowing White to score. Then came the play that was the crux of the whole game; perhaps the entire Series.

With men on first and second Goslin bunted in front of the plate. DeLancey pounced on it, took in the situation in one swift glance and elected to try for a force play at third. As Cochrane slid in, umpire Brick Owens' hand went up in the air for the out, and the Tigers went wild.

Cochrane, Owens and half the Tiger team stood bunched around third base, arguing hotly. "I beat the throw a mile!" the Tiger pilot screamed, red-faced. "You're out!" Owens repeated coldly. Martin stood on the bag, grinning silently.

The umpire's decision stood, of course, but forever after, Cochrane proclaimed that he was safe. "I'd stake my career that I beat the throw," he maintained. "I was never surer of any play."

But he was out, and instead of bases loaded and nobody out there were men on first and second with one out. Thus only the tying run came in a moment later when Greenberg singled to center. Paul held, and the game went into the seventh inning tied 3–3.

Again it was the Gas House Gang's weak-hitting shortstop who began the rally. This time it was the winning one. He rocked Rowe for a double, his first Series extra-base hit, and scored when Paul followed with a single to right.

Final score, Cardinals 4, Detroit 3, and the Series was tied at three games apiece. The stage was set for the final act. It was just like the Gas House Gang to wind it up the way they did—wild, funny, exciting, and history-making.

And, as usual, Dizzy Dean led the way.

He began the day's incredible events, as he always did, with his inimitable needling of the opposition. He stood to one side, watching the Tigers' submarine-pitching Eldon Auker warm up, then yelled to Cochrane, "He jest won't do, Mickey!"

Though the advantage was the Tigers', playing the final game in their home park, it was the Gas House Gang that brimmed over with confidence. After all, Dizzy was in there pitching; the Tigers had beaten him once, in a close one, but they would never beat him twice. Nobody on the Cardinals even imagined such an eventuality.

114

For two innings the seventh game was a scoreless contest. Then Dizzy came to bat with one out in the third. He rapped Auker's first pitch for a double down the left field line, and stood prancing down off second base yelling to Cochrane, "I tol' you he wouldn't do, Mickey!"

That was just the spark the Gas Housers needed. Martin followed with a bunt single, Rothrock walked and Frisch doubled. At that point Cochrane removed Auker and brought in his ace, Schoolboy Rowe. The chips were down now: there was no tomorrow for which to save his men.

The Gas House Gang was riding high. Rip Collins met Rowe with a single, DeLancey doubled, Durocher singled and Dizzy, up for the second time in the inning, finished Rowe with another single. Seven runs poured in before Hogsett, who had replaced Rowe, could get the third out.

Ahead 7–0, Dizzy began to clown on the mound as though it were an exhibition game, not the climactic contest of the World Series. The Detroit fans, disappointed and humiliated at the sudden Cardinal outburst, began to boo and shout ugly comments at the Gas House Gang. The more Dizzy and the rest made obvious their disdain for the Tigers, the worse the crowd got.

In the sixth inning the pot finally boiled over. With Martin on second and two out, Medwick belted a drive to the right field exit gate. Head down he came barreling around second, took off for third and slid in safely, spikes high. Owen came up out of the dust with his left

115

foot dripping blood. Swearing and sputtering he stepped on Medwick's ankle. Medwick kicked him in the chest. In a moment the two men were trading punches. Umpire Bill Klem and coach Mike Gonzalez broke them up quickly as the huge Tiger crowd thundered its anger.

When Medwick trotted out to left field moments later, he was greeted by a wave of jeers, quickly followed by a rain of pop bottles, newspapers, leftovers from lunch boxes, seat cushions and even a few chairs. Medwick retreated to the dugout until the litter was cleared and the crowd silenced.

Now they were ready to play ball again and Medwick ran out to left field once more. The crowd was waiting. Another torrent of abuse and garbage was hurled at him. Again he fled to the safety of the dugout.

From his box behind third base, Commissioner Landis stood up and called for a hasty conference. He summoned the four umpires, Medwick, Owen and the rival managers. Quickly he decided. "Frisch," he said, "you'll have to take Medwick out of the game."

"But why should I?" demanded Frisch. "It ain't his fault the fans have gone crazy."

"Because I said so," stormed Landis. "Because I want to see this game finished sometime today."

It seemed grossly unfair to the Cardinals, and indeed most of the sports writers criticized Landis in print for the decision. But he confided later that he wouldn't have done it if the Cardinals hadn't been so far ahead.

In any case Medwick was out and Chuck Fullis replaced him.

The Cardinals rolled on against the Tigers' relief staff. Cochrane threw in pinch hitters at every opportunity in a desperate attempt to avert disaster. Dizzy, grinning and lobbing the ball teasingly to the plate, continued to pitch shutout ball.

The score was 11–0 when the Tigers came up for their last chance. Dizzy got the first man, walked the next, then gave up a single. That brought up Greenberg. Dizzy had twice struck out the vaunted slugger in the early innings. Now he called out to Cochrane, "What, no pinch hitter for this guy?"

Greenberg's face turned purple. He looked as though he would have liked to break his bat over Dizzy's head. Dizzy just grinned at him, then threw two fast balls waist high right over the heart of the plate. Greenberg swung and missed both times.

On the mound Dizzy doubled over with laughter, hiding his face with his glove. Frisch came running in from second base, his face tight with anger. "Cut out the fooling," he said, "we got a lot at stake."

Durocher, who had come to the mound with Frisch, overheard. "Aw, c'mon, Frank, let the guy have his fun," the shortstop said. "What's the matter with you? We're leading eleven–nothing."

"Yeah, well he loses this guy he's through!" Frisch snarled.

"You wouldn't do that, Dutchman," Dizzy protested. "Not with all them people lookin' on and listenin' on the radio."

117

"I got four pitchers warming up in the bullpen," Frisch replied. "Just try me."

Dizzy stared at him in disbelief. "The Dutchman's lost his mind," he said to Durocher. But he turned around and fogged a third strike past the frustrated Greenberg. He was so sure of that pitch, he contemptuously turned his back on home plate as soon as the ball left his hand.

A moment later Owen forced Rogell and the World Series was over—the Gas House Gang were World's Champions!

In the bedlam of the clubhouse later, Dizzy sat in front of his locker, twisting the tail of a blown-up rubber tiger for the benefit of the photographers. "Me and Paul done it again!" he was shouting. "Jest like I always told everybody."

Nobody could deny it. They had won forty-nine of the Cardinals' ninety-five victories for the season and all of the World Series victories—two each. On top of that, Dizzy was voted the Most Valuable Player award in the National League by the Baseball Writers Association, and the Year's Outstanding Athlete in a nation-wide Associated Press poll of sports writers and editors. Dizzy won the latter award over such renowned athletes as golfer Lawson Little, who came in second, boxer Max Baer, tennis champ Fred Perry of England and world's record mile runner Glenn Cunningham.

Yet in the clubhouse celebration manager Frisch said to him: "Anybody with your stuff should have won forty games this year instead of a measly thirty. You loaf, that's the trouble. Thirty games! You should be ashamed of yourself!"

Dizzy looked after him curiously as he walked away. "You know, I really like the Dutchman," he said quietly, "but he worries all the time."

The vague irritation left behind by Frisch with his half-joking remark was not the first incident of its kind. Early in the Series he had confided to shortstop Durocher that he was feeling kind of tired, the years were catching up with him. "Do me a favor and play a little closer to second," he said. "Give me a hand."

He forgot for the moment that Durocher was a born Gas Houser.

"Get yourself a wheel chair if you can't cover your ground," Leo snarled at him. "I'm not gonna make myself look bad so you can look good!"

It did not portend well for the Cardinals' future.

11 ●●●●●●

Dizzy always admitted it, and the fact came to the fore soon after the 1934 World Series—he wanted to make the most money he could as quickly as he could from baseball. Salaries weren't very high in those years; he got only $7,500 pitching one of the greatest seasons in baseball history (Paul's salary while winning nineteen games was $3,000). So he tried to cash in on his popularity elsewhere.

In this his wife Pat was squarely behind him. She was, in fact, responsible for most of his business affairs, including his contracts with the Cardinals. "Somebody has to know something about business," she remarked cheerfully that fall. "Baseball strategy is Dizzy's department. Practical sense is mine. I know how the money is to be got and what to do with it. After all, a baseball player's life is short. Three big years are all he can count on. I've heard cheers change to jeers all in one breath. The higher you go, the harder you fall."

"You think, then, that Dizzy may have reached his peak and is on his way down?" a sports writer asked her.

"No. But when the crowds start booing Dizzy instead

of cheering him I want him to be able to retire grace-
fully with money in his pockets."

To get some of that money "Dizzy and Daffy" became
a kind of vaudeville team. They toured the semipro baseball circuit from Brooklyn to as far west as Milwaukee.
They picked up five thousand for pitching two innings
each in Chicago and a thousand dollars each for pitching
for the famed Brooklyn Bushwicks against the Black
Yankees of the Negro League. Dizzy lost that game on
a balk, and complained with wonder. "I ain't had a balk
called on me in years, and I have to come to Brooklyn to
lose a game with one against a semipro team. It's down-
right humiliatin'."

Between exhibition games the Deans made public appearances, speaking at dinners, on radio, on the vaudeville stage. For the most part the quiet Paul let Dizzy
carry the speaking chores. The elder brother found that
speaking in public was as natural to him as pitching.
"Why I jest go out there like they was all reg'lar folks
from back home and I tell 'em a few stories," he said.
"Easy as eatin' possum pie."

Back in Brooklyn in November they made a two-reel
movie, a short feature called "Dizzy and Daffy" in which
they portrayed members of a team called the Farmers.
It was supposed to be a comedy, and it turned out that
way, but the producers would have been more successful,
perhaps produced a classic, had they secretly filmed the
brothers when they were fooling around between scenes.

One day Paul began a guessing game with Dizzy. He
went through pitching motions, imitating the style of

121

Paul Derringer of the Reds. "Now you have to guess who that was," he said.

"It might be Jess Haines," Dizzy guessed. "I know it weren't no Dean though."

"Why that was Derringer," Paul said. "Now see if you can guess this one." He went through another complete delivery, this time copying Lon Warneke of the Cubs.

"Mungo!" Dizzy said brightly.

"No," Paul said disgustedly. "You been in the league three years already and you don't know Warneke's style? I'm surprised at you, Brother."

"Well, they probably don't know mine neither," Dizzy said defensively. "Anyways, we better play a different game before you try to copy Fat Freddie Fitzsimmons and fall down."

When Paul's arm began to feel sore from the postseason pitching, Dizzy cut the tour short and headed for St. Louis to negotiate his 1935 contract. "I'm very reasonable," he said. "Take some and leave some is my motto. I want twenty-five thousand dollars next year and Paul wants fifteen."

"You made a lot of money barnstorming," he was reminded by a sports writer. "You think Breadon will count that against you?"

"Don't see why," Dizzy replied. "We never did nothing to hurt ourselves for the Cards. Fact is, a promoter feller offered me ten thousand dollars to wrestle with Man Mountain Dean—no relation of mine o' course—and I turned him down cold. Probably coulda beat him

122

too if'n we wrestled mountain style, but I didn't want to hurt my arm."

The Cardinal management was far from ready to sign the Deans, however. A two-day conference with president Sam Breadon was cordial, but unpromising. "You're too high," the St. Louis executive said calmly.

"Not a penny less," Dizzy retorted. He left for Bradenton, Florida, where, in a section named "Deanville" by the town's city council, he had a winter home.

Negotiations continued by phone and by mail. Early in December Breadon visited Dizzy in Bradenton, but several days of conversation proved futile, and he returned to St. Louis. More phone calls followed, until on December 6 the Cardinals and Dizzy announced jointly that he had signed a contract. But trouble started when Dizzy figured out—with Pat's help—exactly how much the Cardinals planned to pay him for pitching and how much for outside activities such as endorsements, which they handled for him. The pitching figure was not what he thought it would be.

"They fooled me!" he exclaimed. "They didn't keep their promise! Well I'm goin' to New York tomorrow to those National League meetings and get this settled once and for all."

To complicate matters further, believing Dizzy had signed and returned his contract, Paul had signed his in Hot Springs, Arkansas, where he was vacationing. But Dizzy refused to allow it. "Paul only thinks he's satisfied," he said. "That's because he got fooled like I did.

123

We stick together. He don't sign if'n I don't, and I do likewise with him."

At New York's Waldorf Hotel, Breadon and Rickey calmly waited for Dizzy's assault. While they busied themselves with other club executives, working out the 1935 schedules, Dizzy let himself be heard by the willing ears of the sports writers.

"If'n the Cardinals don't think I'm worth twenty-five thousand, then they oughtta sell me or trade me," he said. "I'll play for anybody but the Braves or the Phillies."

None of the club executives believed the Cardinals had any intentions of selling Dizzy, but just in case, the Giants' Bill Terry said he was interested. "I'd give a hundred thousand dollars for Dizzy this minute," he said.

Conferences in New York failed to settle the dispute, however. It dragged out to St. Louis. First Rickey talked with Dizzy, then Breadon. The battle lasted until early February, when terms were finally agreed on in the Cardinals' office. Dizzy didn't get his twenty-five thousand but did get more than the seventeen thousand five hundred that was once the Cardinals' final offer.

The contract was signed ceremoniously for the benefit of the St. Louis sports writers and news photographers. "We're both satisfied," said Breadon.

"That's right," said Dizzy. "And to prove that me and Sam are the best of friends I'll let you take a picture of me with my arm around Sam's neck. Let's shake on it, eh, Sam?"

Breadon smiled. "Sure. I have to congratulate you on that contract. It calls for a lot of money."

"Yeah, but I'm worth it," Dizzy said.

If the Cardinals thought, with a sigh of relief, that their extroverted pitcher was now in hibernation until spring training, they were soon disabused of such notions. His off-season fireworks had a couple of large firecrackers yet to be exploded.

Several weeks after the settlement of the contract dispute, it was announced in the newspapers that the incomparable, the immortal Babe Ruth had been signed by the Boston Braves as assistant manager and pinch hitter. For some reason Dizzy immediately and loudly expressed his resentment of the move. Considering Ruth's immense popularity it was an opinion not calculated to endear Dizzy to a great many people. But he thought it, and when he thought something he said it so everybody could hear it.

"He made all his money in the American League," he declared. "Why don't he stay there? Why does he have to come to the National League and maybe eventually knock a nice feller like Bill McKechnie out of a manager's job. Why couldn't the American League find a place for him now that his playin' days are done? I resent his comin' here, and I think practically every player in the league'll feel the same way."

Surprised by the uproar against him following his tirade against Ruth, and advised privately that it would do him great harm to let it stand, Dizzy hastened to amend his statement.

"I guess maybe I popped off too fast, and I was wrong," he admitted to a sports writer. "But I want to explain what I meant, and you'll see that it ain't as bad as it sounded at first. You know I ain't always the best at talkin' sense. But first of all even the Babe'll tell you that me and him are good friends. Why we hunt together in the winter, and he's given me some good advice. Whatever I said against him I never meant personal."

"What do you mean, 'personal'?" the writer asked.

"Well I guess I was more mad at the American League than anything. What's the matter with them, letting a great guy like the Babe get outa their league? Couldn't nobody make him an assistant manager there? And then at first I thought he was coming in to take away Bill McKechnie's job. I know different now, and I'm sorry if the Babe thought I was talkin' against him.

"In fact, first chance I get I'm gonna walk up to the big guy and tell him how great I think he is and how we're all pulling for him to have a good year. Yes, sir, tell the Babe for me that I'm on the square for him." Then Dizzy grinned mischievously. "Besides, I can't afford to put the blast on a hitter like Ruth. He might ram the ball down my throat one day."

Quiet settled down once more over the turbulent waters that ebbed and flowed around Dizzy Dean—but not for long. Spring training was just days away when he was suddenly summoned to the Chicago offices of the baseball commissioner. Operating on information from

126

various sources, Landis called a hearing on charges that Dizzy had accepted a bonus from Dick Slack, an East St. Louis furniture dealer and avid baseball fan, for signing his 1935 contract with the Cardinals. Allegedly, Slack gave him the money to keep peace in the Cardinal family.

The charges were serious. Landis made a formal affair of the hearing. He sat behind his huge, paper-strewn desk and ordered Dizzy to pull up a chair facing him.

"Now," began Landis, "state your name and the team you play for."

Dizzy stared at him in amazement. "Why you know me, Judge," he said. "You seen me pitch lots of times."

"This is a formal hearing," Landis said patiently. "You must state your name and team for the record."

"Jerome Dean, but they call me 'Dizzy,'" he said meekly. "I pitch with the St. Louis Cardinals."

"Now what's this all about?" Landis demanded. "What about this bonus?"

"Nothin' to it, Judge, so far as I know," Dizzy replied. "Sure, I got a contract for five thousand dollars with Slack. But it's for radio work and personal appearances advertising his store. That's all. He's a pretty nice guy, Judge. And he's got lots of dough." From his jacket pocket he extracted the contract and handed it across the desk to the commissioner.

Landis glanced at it, then looked up at Dizzy. "Just answer my question. Doesn't it interest you to know where 'lots of dough' comes from?"

"Why sure it does, Judge."

"What about this hundred dollars a game for every

127

game you won last year Slack was supposed to have paid you?"

"I can't understand how that story got printed," Dizzy said. "Last year it was the same deal. I got money for radio and personal appearances at the store."

Landis then began a long speech about the dangers of accepting money from persons outside baseball. Dizzy interrupted him. "Say, listen, Judge, supposin' a guy comes up and hands you three or four thousand dollars. What about it?"

"People just don't go around doing that," Landis said. Then, waving his finger over his head in warning, he continued, "If anybody offers you that amount of money 'just for doing nothing,' you kick his teeth in, or promise me that you'll grab a baseball bat and hit him on the head."

Dizzy sat in awe at the commissioner's sudden outburst. "Yes, sir," he said quietly, and left the hearing room, absolved, but chastened. "For a while there the Judge sounded jest like the preacher back home when I was a kid," he said later.

Spring came and with it the preseason fireworks died out. Dizzy was ready to pitch again, to lead the Gas House Gang to another World's Championship. But, just to prepare the Cardinals for what was to come, he fired two more small firecrackers before opening day. At an exhibition tour he missed a train, and a game, and was fined a hundred dollars by Frisch. He paid it without protest this time, but he was obviously unhappy.

Three days later he announced that after two more years he was quitting baseball.

"I'm gonna hang up my uniform and take it easy," he said. "Maybe go into some business. Pat's been savin' our money, and we can do all right without baseball."

Nobody took him seriously, but in the upper echelons of the Cardinal organization worried frowns began to appear. Too much had been happening. Too many whispers were being overheard. Dissension seemed to be threatening the Gas House Gang.

"The team better get off to a fast start," one executive said anxiously. "Or there's liable to be an explosion."

The fuse smoldered during the early weeks of the season. Tex Carleton was traded to the Cubs. Paul Dean's arm, which had been hurt on the Deans' postseason tour, remained sore, affecting his pitching considerably. Catcher Bill DeLancey was taken sick. Durocher and Frisch continued their silent but serious feud around second base. The Gas House Gang didn't seem to have the old drive. Even Dizzy's fast ball seemed to have lost a bit of its hop. By the first week in June he had won six games, but lost four. The Cardinals were bogged down near the bottom of the first division.

The explosion came on June 5, in Pittsburgh.

For two innings Dizzy and Pirate hurler Cy Blanton pitched scoreless ball. The Cardinals then jumped on Blanton for two runs in the third, but the Pirates came back and blasted Dizzy for four. Never a good loser, Dizzy was burning as he went up to bat in the fourth,

129

and when he was called out on strikes he stalked back to the bench, yelling at the plate umpire.

When he reached the dugout Medwick said to him: "Lay off the ump and bear down in there. You'll be better off."

Dizzy stared at Ducky. "Whatta you mean, bear down?" he said angrily. "I'll punch you right on your Hungarian beezer!"

Medwick bounded from the dugout and grabbed a bat from the rack near the water cooler. Dizzy came up after him. In another moment they were at each other in front of the dugout in full view of all the fans. Quickly the Cardinal players separated them before any serious blows were struck.

Manager Frisch was livid with rage. "I'll take care of you later!" he hissed at Dizzy.

The rest of the game was a shambles. The Pirates rapped Dizzy for five more runs before he was lifted for a pinch hitter in the seventh inning. The Cardinals lost, 9–5, Dizzy's fifth loss against six victories, and in the clubhouse afterward Frisch pulled out all the stops.

"You've been getting on the umpires and the other guys here long enough," he said bitterly, "—shooting off your mouth about how they're quitting on you. Well I say your bad record's your own fault. You're the guy who's lying down on the job. You think just because you're Dizzy Dean you can groove the ball in there and everybody's gonna fold up. I tell you to pitch one way to a guy like Arky Vaughan and you do it your own way. So what happens? He beats you twice, just like he did today. No one guy can win a pennant, Dizzy, and it's about time you learned it. Now I'm warning you. Another outburst like today, any more remarks about guys quitting on you, and I'll fine you five thousand dollars and suspend you from the club!"

During Frisch's tirade Dizzy stood quietly in front of his locker. He wasn't smiling now. When Frisch stopped he said evenly, "If you're all through, Frank, I jest wanna tell you somethin'. You can say whatever you want about me, but if'n you can thank anybody for the job you got as manager you can thank me, and you know it."

Though the explosion widened the cracks that were beginning to show in the structure of the Gas House Gang, strangely enough it also had the temporary effect of fusing them as a team. Angry at each other, at Frisch, at their standing in the league, they broke out in June and began winning. Especially Dizzy. Becoming once again virtually unbeatable, he regained a measure of his old clowning self on the mound. Never again was he as gay and as loose as in the madcap days of 1934—none of the Gas House Gang were—but occasionally, not often or blatantly enough to risk Frisch's ever-increasing irritability, he lapsed into a conservative version of the old Dizzy Dean.

One day in July he revealed that he still had some showmanship in him when challenged by the Giants' Bill Terry. The New Yorkers' manager had been needling him all season. "You don't have that old fog ball any more, Diz!" Terry jabbed at him continually. And

Dizzy took it. But his patience had its limits, and now, leading the Giants by an 8–0 score, he saw his chance to silence Terry. Three times during the game he had gotten Terry out, but he wanted to humiliate him, show him that though more subdued on the mound he was still the best pitcher in baseball.

Terry, however, was sixth in the batting order as the Giants came to bat in the ninth inning. Dizzy grinned. Here was just the kind of spot he had been waiting for all afternoon. He retired the first two batters, then called out to Terry, "All right, wise guy, I'm gonna give you your big chance now."

Deliberately he walked the next three batters to load the bases. Frisch fumed, but said nothing. Terry stepped up to the plate, waving his bat menacingly. "I'll pin your ears back!" he shouted to Dizzy.

"I don't have the fast one no more, eh?" Dizzy shouted back. "Here comes three right down the pipe, let's see you hit one!"

Dizzy wound up. Terry cocked his bat. The fast ball came through the middle. Terry swung and missed.

Grinning, Dizzy stood on the mound, taking his time, rubbing up the ball. Terry dug his spikes in deeper, and cocked his bat again. Dizzy wound up and fired another fast ball over the heart of the plate. Terry swung and missed again!

He stepped out of the box now, bent and scooped up a handful of dirt, rubbed it between his palms. His eyes were glittering slits as he stepped back into the batter's box. His knuckles were white from squeezing the bat so tightly.

Dizzy grinned at him disdainfully. "Here comes number three, Billy boy!" he called and put all he had behind another fast ball. Terry swung desperately—but missed again for strike three!

Dizzy, satisfaction gained, was walking off the mound before the ball even reached the plate.

Such moments were all too few, however. The Gas House Gang was just not the old high-spirited crew anymore. Although they led the league all through that summer of 1935, something had gone out of them. Dissension and dissatisfaction gnawed away at their morale. There were no more hillbilly songs in the dugout, no more practical jokes. The umpire baiting now was serious rather than part of the act.

Despite it all the Cardinals looked like a sure bet for a repeat pennant as the race entered its final month. But the Chicago Cubs put together an amazing winning streak of twenty-one straight games in September to nose them out.

Despite his slow start, Dizzy came back with another great season. He again led the league in victories, with twenty-eight; in strikeouts, with one hundred ninety-five; and in innings pitched, with three hundred twenty-four.

12 ••••••

The disintegration of the Gas House Gang continued through the 1936 season. By 1937 it was virtually complete. Catcher DeLancey was gone, the victim of tuberculosis. Orsatti and Rothrock were released. Hallahan was traded to Cincinnati in 1936 and Rip Collins to the Cubs. And "Me and Paul" became virtually a memory. Though "Daffy" had again won nineteen games in 1935, he had lost twelve. As that season had waned, his sore arm had become worse. Finally, in 1936 he was forced to quit in mid-season with a five won, five lost record.

Dizzy tried to make light of it, but there were tears in his eyes the day he said good-bye to his brother in the Cardinal clubhouse. "You'll be back, Paul," he said. "Jest give that ol' arm a little time to rest, and you'll be right back here with me, just like it used to be."

But Paul knew the truth. "I think I've had it all, Diz," he said, trying hard, for his brother's sake, to hide the hurt he was feeling inside. "I got no complaints. You know, I never was as good as you always made out I was anyhow. Sometimes I used to think I was winnin' ball

134

games jest because you had scared them other guys into thinkin' I was as good as you."

"Shucks, Paul, you was better. Why I was just a busher compared to you. You jest had hard luck, is all."

After a season's rest Paul did try a comeback, but he was never an effective pitcher again. He actually lingered in baseball until 1943, pitching mostly in relief, winning a few games, losing a few, capitalizing on his past reputation and the drawing card he knew he was as Dizzy's brother. He bounced around from the Cardinals to the minor leagues to the Giants and finally to the Cubs. In his best year after 1936 he won just four games for the 1940 Giants. In 1943 he retired to look after his real estate interests in Texas.

Dizzy in 1936 won twenty-six and lost twelve. He began the season sensationally, by mid-June compiling thirteen wins with only two losses. But when Paul was forced to quit he was called on to take up the slack. Always a hard worker, he suddenly became practically a one-man pitching staff. Frisch worked him regularly every third day and in relief between starts. Uncomplaining, because in truth he would have asked to pitch every day were it humanly possible, he nevertheless was bound to lose some of his effectiveness. He won thirteen but lost ten for the balance of the season, appearing in a total of fifty-one games.

As for the Cardinals, they slipped a notch further down in the league standings, finishing third behind the Giants and Cubs.

135

For a brief period, in the spring of 1937, a touch of harmony—violent harmony though it was—gave promise of better things for the Gas House Gang. In Florida for spring training, Dizzy got into a fight with two sports writers. For some time he had been fretting about the writings of one of the men. "I don't mind too much what he says about me," he said to one of his teammates, "but I don't like when he keeps sayin' that my wife tells me everything I should do. It ain't right, bringin' Pat into it."

The two men had it out in a hotel lobby one evening. It began as a verbal battle. As it got louder the writer was joined by one from another newspaper. Several of the Cardinals gathered around. Suddenly there was a shove, a swing, and the men were at each other. The second writer made a move as if to grab Dizzy. This the Gas Housers would not tolerate. Squabbles among themselves were one thing. But a fist fight against outsiders was another, especially when the odds appeared unfair for one of them.

Medwick, who a year earlier had been ready to club Dizzy with a bat, moved in to help him. He hit the second writer a left hook to the cheek, and in another moment the rest of the Cardinals piled into the fray, burying the two writers in an avalanche of blows.

The fight was broken up by outsiders before anyone was seriously hurt. No charges were brought. No fines were imposed by Frisch, who was secretly delighted. It was the first sign of solidarity by the Gas House Gang in a long time. The Cardinals' manager was almost ready to forgive Dizzy all his past sins for inadvertently bringing the Gas Housers together.

"If only he won't upset the apple cart now," Frisch said to himself. "I'd like to see one season without any big hassles."

Knowing the temperament of his pitcher the way he did, Frisch should never have dreamed the impossible. In little more than a month Dizzy jumped feet first into the biggest "hassle" of his battle-scarred career.

On June 19, as Dizzy warmed up for a game in St. Louis against the New York Giants, umpire George Barr reminded him that the balk rule was now in effect. "I'm telling you because I mean to enforce it," the umpire cautioned him. "I know it never has been before, but we got orders from today on to call it when we see it. Now remember, when you got a man on first or second and you go into your stretch, you got to come down to a complete stop and let the ball touch the glove before starting to pitch."

Dizzy nodded his understanding and continued to warm up.

Twice during the game, however, the umpire had to warn him that he was committing a balk. Finally he told Mickey Owen, the Cardinals' new catcher, that on the next balk he was going to call it and penalize Dizzy.

Owen delivered the message. Dizzy ignored it. In the middle of a Giant rally he committed a balk. Barr stepped out in front of the plate and called it. Giant runners on first and second advanced a base. On the mound Dizzy sputtered and turned red in the face. Angrily he threw his next pitch high and inside to batter Jimmy Ripple. Ripple hit the dirt just in time as the ball sailed where his head had been a moment before.

In a flash Ripple was up and rushed furiously at the mound. Dizzy came charging in to meet him. Players from both dugouts bounded onto the field, and in seconds a full-scale riot was in progress. It took a half-hour for the managers, coaches and park police to separate the players. As usual in such field melees there was more motion than actual damage. When peace was restored, the Giants took advantage of the balk by rallying for three runs to win the ball game.

The following day National League President Ford Frick fined Dizzy and Ripple fifty dollars each for fighting. That appeared to end the matter. But Dizzy didn't like to be fined. Furthermore he didn't like the notion that umpires would be enforcing the long-standing but long-ignored balk rule. Finally he was hopping mad at losing the game to the Giants because of Barr's balk call.

A week later he appeared one evening at a meeting of businessmen at the First Presbyterian Church of Belleville, Illinois. As guest speaker he regaled the assembly with his droll baseball stories.

The next day a story appeared in the Belleville *Daily Advocate* quoting Dizzy as saying that Ford Frick and umpire George Barr were "the two biggest crooks in baseball."

These were most serious charges. If Dizzy made them, as the paper claimed, it was a grievous slap in the face to both men and to baseball in general. Far more was at stake here than a fist fight between players or insulting an umpire on the playing field or even questionable testimonials for business enterprises. The honesty and integrity of baseball itself were in question.

Immediately upon learning of the newspaper article Frick suspended Dizzy indefinitely, "for conduct detrimental to the best interests of baseball."

Dizzy got the notice next day along with a prepared letter of apology he was ordered to sign. One act for which he was to apologize concerned throwing "beanballs" in the Giant game that started the entire chain of events. Frick, when questioned, declared that the suspension was not merely because of the statements attributed to Dizzy, but because of a long series of incidents culminating in the riot at Sportsman's Park.

In the clubhouse at Ebbets Field in Brooklyn when he was handed the letter, Dizzy read the suspension notice and apology. Frick also asked that he appear in New York with manager Frisch for a hearing.

Dizzy showed the letters disgustedly to a sports writer. "I'll tell Frick just what I think of him when I get to New York," he said. "I'm so mad I'm gonna refuse to play in the All-Star game this year."

"Diz, did you say those things about Barr and Frick?" he was asked.

"Would I say things like that in a church?" Dizzy replied. "Sure, I said plenty about the balk rule, it being unfair and putting an extra burden on a pitcher's arm. And I'll say it again. What do fellers like Frick know about what a ballplayer can or can't do? I tell you baseball's becoming so soft they'll be making us wear tennis shoes next so's we won't hurt anybody!"

Two days later the hearing took place in the New York office of the National League President. Dizzy, Frisch, other Cardinal executives and a dozen reporters crowded into Frick's offices high in the R.C.A. building. When the talks began it became apparent at once that the only issue of importance was Dizzy's alleged accusation that Frick and umpire Barr were crooks. The beanballs and other incidents of rebellion were thrust aside.

"What I want from you, Mr. Dean, is a signed statement that you did not make those remarks," Frick said. "I'm willing to give you the benefit of the doubt."

"I ain't signin' nothin' that has an apology in it," Dizzy said.

Frick handed him a typed statement. "This is a redraft of the note I sent you with the suspension notice. Read it and see if it meets with your approval."

Dizzy looked at the note. "No," he said. "I got here a telegram from nine members of that church I spoke at, saying that I said nothing to hurt baseball. Ain't that good enough?"

This time it was Frick's turn to refuse. "I must have your sworn statement, signed."

"I ain't signin' no apology," Dizzy insisted.

Frick sighed. "I'll have another form prepared. You can choose anybody you like, one of the St. Louis sports writers, for example, and let him approve the statement, let him tell you that it's fair. How would that be?"

"Sounds reasonable," Dizzy said. He chose a friendly

St. Louis newspaperman and left the room while the two men worked on a new statement. In a few moments he was called back, shown the new version. He read it swiftly, but turned angrily and strode into the anteroom shouting to the waiting reporters. "I'm all washed up! The suspension's still on and I'm goin' home. They want me to sign somethin' else, and I came here with the idea I ain't signin' nothin'!"

The writers stampeded into Frick's private office. The league president seemed defeated.

"What can I do?" he said, spreading his hands in a gesture of futility. "I must have documentary evidence from Dean on his denials. That's all there is to it."

Suggestions and opinions flew about the office. Dizzy was still in the outer office, waiting for a decision. Suddenly Frick slammed his hand on the desk. "I got it! I'll tell you what I'll do. If Dean will sit here and answer questions, if the answers are satisfactory, and if you gentlemen of the press will sign the paper, we'll settle this right now."

Dizzy agreed and a stenographer was brought in. The questioning began.

"Mr. Dean," Frick said, "did you make the statement attributed to you that the balk rule was instituted as a direct slap at you and constituted persecution?"

"I did not," said Dizzy.

Frick then asked a series of questions designed to bring out the fact that Dizzy had been properly notified about the new enforcement rule concerning balks.

Then he said, "You have been quoted in the newspapers of Belleville, Illinois, as saying that the president of the National League and umpire George Barr were the two biggest crooks in baseball. The editor of the paper stands by that article. Did you or did you not make that statement?"

"I never said that," said Dizzy emphatically.

Frick nodded his head in satisfaction. He had the questions and answers typed, and the reporters present affixed their signatures as witnesses. Then Frick released a statement of his own to the press, saying in essence that since no official of the league was present when the slurring remarks allegedly were spoken, the president of the league was willing to give Dizzy the benefit of the doubt. His suspension was lifted.

All present started a sigh of relief. But Dizzy wasn't through yet. Suddenly he shook his finger at Frick and said, "Wait a minute. I wanna make a statement. This case ain't over."

Frisch put a hand to his head in anguish. A reporter gasped. "What do you mean, Dizzy?" another asked.

"I mean I'm gonna take this case to Judge Landis. I have been accused of doin' something I didn't do and sayin' something I didn't say."

Frick turned white. He jerked forward in his chair. "Better hold that statement, boys!" he said to the reporters.

"You're makin' a heel outa me and you're the big hero," Dizzy continued, barking at the league president. "I'm gonna take this case right up to the top."

For several moments the entire matter hung in the

balance. But Frick's patience prevailed. "I'm going to ignore Mr. Dean's last remarks," he said. "He answered my questions, which was all I required of him. As far as this office is concerned the case is closed."

The Cardinals were eager enough to get Dizzy back in uniform. Newcomers to the Cardinals such as catcher Mickey Owen and first baseman Johnny Mize were playing fine ball, but as a whole the St. Louis hitting attack was weak. The pitching, too, faltered. Only Dizzy seemed able to win consistently. He returned from his suspension and promptly pitched the Cardinals out of the second division depths to which they had fallen. Taking on four starting assignments in one week to make up for lost time, he dazzled the entire league with his brilliance.

First he tackled the Philadelphia Phillies, beating them 4–0 with a three-hitter. Two days later he beat the Giants, 2–1, batting in the winning run himself with an eighth-inning double. Then he defeated Boston twice in a four-game series, shutting them out the first time, winning 5–3 in the finale.

"Diz may not be the most likable guy in the world," Frisch sighed after the last Boston game, "but he's for sure the best pitcher in the world."

At All-Star time the big right-hander boasted a 12–1 record and was on his way to another great season. Named for the fourth straight time to pitch in the annual classic, Dizzy refused. "I told Frick I wasn't gonna pitch in the All-Star game, and I mean it," he said.

"For Heaven's sake how long you gonna carry a

grudge?" Frisch asked him. "That whole thing is over. Forget it, willya?"

"I got a memory like a Arkansas mule," Dizzy said.

"And a stubborn streak to match," Frisch fumed. "Now before you start another fight let's announce that you're going, willya? Don't you want to pitch in front of President Roosevelt?"

"Yeah, I guess that would be kinda fun," Dizzy agreed. "All right, Dutchman, I'll play in the All-Star game."

For once in Dizzy's life the right decision turned out to be a wrong one—a momentously wrong one.

With the popular President Franklin D. Roosevelt on hand to view the All-Star classic from a special box seat, a huge crowd jammed the Washington ball park on July 7. Dizzy was introduced to the President, laughingly exchanging autographs with him, then went to the mound for the National League to pitch to Earl Averill of the Cleveland Indians, leadoff American League batter.

Averill took a strike, then a ball. Dizzy came back with a fast ball just over the knees over the inside corner. Averill swung, cracked a low line drive right back at the pitcher's mound. Dizzy never had a chance to lower his glove. The ball smashed squarely into the front of his left foot and caromed off. He hobbled after the ball but it was easy for Averill to beat it out for a single.

Dizzy limped painfully around the mound for a few moments, then sat down. The trainer hurried out, followed quickly by Frisch. "It hurts like all dickens," Dizzy said, his eyes squinting with pain. "My toes feel like they was squashed."

The trainer began to remove Dizzy's left shoe. "No, don't take it off," he protested. "You do that and the whole foot'll swell up."

"I'll have to take it off in the clubhouse anyway," the trainer said, motioning for a stretcher.

"Clubhouse nothin'," Dizzy said. "I ain't gonna quit in front of all these people and the President of the United States. Jest help me up."

Over the protests of Frisch and the trainer, Dizzy got to his feet. He waved them back to the dugout, indicating to the plate umpire that he would like to try a few warm-up pitches to test his foot. It was obvious even to those in the grandstand that it was sheer agony for him to put pressure on the left foot. But he remained in the game. The crowd gave him a huge ovation as he resumed pitching.

Dizzy delivered his three innings of pitching, the maximum allowed a pitcher under All-Star rules. He pitched with his body bathed in perspiration from the pain, with his eyes cloudy from it—and his shoulder aching from the strain of trying to ease up off that left foot. But he held the American Leaguers scoreless.

In the clubhouse later, allowing the trainer to cut away his shoe, he learned with regret that his successor, Carl Hubbell of the Giants, had been knocked out of the box. By the time the game was over, the American League victors by 8–3, Dizzy was in the hospital. The big toe on his left foot was broken.

He hobbled around, a splint on the toe, for ten days. In that time the Cardinals lost eight games, dropping from first place contention to fifth place, eleven games behind the league-leading Giants.

Frisch was desperate. He had never let on, but in the Medwick fight back in 1935 Dizzy had hit home when he said the manager's job rode on his shoulders. What success the Gas House Gang had achieved was easily traceable to his superman efforts. No matter what other problems he caused, Dizzy served as the backbone of the Cardinal pitching staff, and thus the team.

With the depths of the second division yawning behind him and a Sunday double-header at Boston staring him in the face, Frisch asked Dizzy to pitch.

"I ain't ready yet," Dizzy said. "But you're the manager. You want me to pitch, I pitch."

From the first warm-up toss he knew something was wrong. Not only did the splint on his toe get in the way, but the pain was like a hot needle when he turned his left foot in the follow-through. He wanted badly to pitch, however. He didn't want anyone to think he was shirking his pitching duties just when he was needed the most.

Dizzy compensated for the immobility of his left foot by using his arm and shoulder more with the pitch. The foot ached less, but the new, unnatural delivery brought unused muscles into play, putting a strain on the shoulder joint. For six innings he labored in torture until he hardly knew which hurt him more, the broken toe or his right shoulder.

He held on, protecting a small lead, until his arm went numb in the middle of the seventh inning. He had no

146

THE DIZZY DEAN STORY

feeling in the tips of his fingers. He threw a few pitches with nothing on the ball, hoping to fool the hitters, but they soon caught on and knocked him out of the box.

He tried again and was knocked out. And again. Frisch wouldn't give up on him; Dizzy refused to give up on himself. He was good for a few innings, then the soreness came. After that the numbness. Finally the deluge of hits. The toe healed, but it left behind a far more serious ailment. Too many innings had been pitched, too many pitches hurled awkwardly, favoring the injured foot.

Dizzy won just one game after the All-Star injury, a 9–7 slugfest, lasting just long enough to get credit for the victory. He lost nine others until he and the Cardinals finally conceded late in August that it was time to have the club surgeon examine the shoulder thoroughly.

"Bursitis of the right shoulder," the doctor reported back. "I'm afraid Dizzy is through for the season."

The Gas House Gang was wheezing its last gasp. The Cardinals finished fourth in 1937, just six percentage points out of the second division. And another member of the original Gang was sacrified. Leo Durocher, the peppery shortstop, his unpublicized, quiet feud with manager Frisch growing more bitter by the season, was traded to the Brooklyn Dodgers.

At least the Number One Gas Houser of them all was still left, Cardinal fans said to each other when Dizzy Dean reported for spring training in 1938. The condition of his sore shoulder was still uncertain after a winter's complete rest and treatment. But at least he was back, and after only a small salary dispute.

The training season did not go well, however. The bursitis was aggravated when he pitched, inflaming the shoulder. He was able to throw perhaps half a game with something like his old speed, then the arm went bad.

Just before opening day in St. Louis he was scheduled to pitch an exhibition game against the Browns. "Just a couple of innings," Frisch said, "to see how you do. I'd still like to start you opening day."

The morning of the exhibition game Dizzy was met at the clubhouse door by Clarence Rowland, a scout for the Chicago Cubs. Rowland grabbed his arm. "Well, Diz, you belong to us now," the scout said.

Dizzy didn't recognize him. He thought the scout was just a Cardinal fan. "I'll see you later, bud," he said, and stepped past him through the clubhouse door.

Inside was a crowd of newspapermen and photographers. Dizzy headed for his locker, wondering what was going on. The newspapermen wondered, too. They had been told only that an important announcement was to be made.

As Dizzy began to remove his street clothes, Branch Rickey came over to him. Draping an arm around his shoulder the Cardinal vice president called for silence.

"We just want to say that we've made a deal with the Cubs, and we have traded this man here—"

A great shout of surprise drowned him out. He motioned once more for silence. "We don't want you players to feel we're letting you down because we've got a man to replace him, and we'll still win the pennant."

Bewildered by the sudden announcement, Dizzy stood in front of his locker, his shirt half unbuttoned, Rickey's arm still on his shoulder. Flash bulbs popped. Reporters jumped for telephones. Pepper Martin, just a towel around his hips, his hair still wet and matted from the shower, stood on a chair and yelled for quiet. "I wanna make a speech too," he said. "Mr. Rickey, we appreciate you coming in to tell us what you've done and that we ain't going to be too bad off even when Diz here goes, and that you still want us to win the pennant. We're all for you and we'll win, too."

Rickey beamed. The reporters then asked Dizzy what he had to say. "Well, I jest want to say to Mr. Rickey that I predicted we'd win the flag right here in St. Louis. But now that I'm gone we'll win it in Chicago, and don't worry I'll see to it that you get a ticket to the World Series."

Dizzy wasted no time checking out. He gathered his personal belongings in a duffel bag, shook hands all around, and left. The difficult parting was with his brother Paul, who was being given a chance for a comeback with the Cardinals.

"Shucks, it don't seem right, me goin' and you stayin'," Dizzy said to him. "It's really only been a few years, but it seems like we've been workin' together a lifetime. I sure hope we never have to pitch against each other."

"If'n we do I'll beat your brains out, Diz," said Paul, forcing a smile.

Dizzy laughed and clapped his brother on the shoulder. "I'll bet you would at that," he said.

A clubhouse full of players, Cardinal executives and newspapermen stood silently for a long moment when the clubhouse door swung shut behind him.

It struck home to all of them. This was the end of the Gas House Gang.

13 ••••••

The Cardinals got pitchers Clyde Shoun, Curt Davis, outfielder Tuck Stainback and $185,000 by trading Dizzy. The Cubs got a pitcher who was once the best in baseball but whose value now was very much in doubt. However, manager Charley Grimm was optimistic. "Maybe Dizzy'll win only eighteen games for us. Maybe only fifteen. But he'll be a lot of help. I won't say the addition of a single pitcher will make us a pennant winner, but the psychology of having a guy like Dizzy around helps a lot."

For once Dizzy himself did no predicting. "I got to see how I can pitch first," he said.

He felt strange in his Cub uniform. Joining the team in Cincinnati he opened the clubhouse door at Crosley Field onto a new world, in effect. There were new faces, new personalities to adjust to, new routines to learn, new friends to make. There was at least one familiar face in the locker room, however, to make things a bit easier. Old Gas Houser Rip Collins was the Cub first baseman.

He introduced Dizzy around. The beefy red-faced man with the cigar was catcher Gabby Hartnett. There were

151

Stan Hack, third baseman; Billy Jurges, shortstop; Billy Herman, second baseman; Tony Lazzeri, former Yankee star, utility infielder; Joe Marty, Phil Cavaretta, Carl Reynolds, outfielders.

Dizzy also met the Cub pitchers, most of whom he had pitched against several times. Bill Lee headed the staff, aided by Clay Bryant, Jack Russell, Larry French, Charley Root and another former member of the Gas House Gang, Tex Carleton. It was virtually the same team that had beaten the Cardinals out of the pennant in 1935. After two subsequent years of near misses, the Cubs hoped Dizzy could help bring the flag back to Wrigley Field.

Just two days after reporting, Grimm—known as "Jolly Cholly" around the league—gave Dizzy his first chance at Crosley Field. Catcher Hartnett worked him carefully, calling for a great many slow curves and change-up pitches, trying to pace him. For seven innings Dizzy looked something like his old self—not as fast but smooth and confident. Behind him, led by Hartnett's homer and two doubles by Collins, the Cubs built up a 7–2 lead.

In the eighth inning the shoulder began to stiffen. A sharp single and a walk gave him warning. It was an effort to control the ball. When he let the Cincinnati pitcher, Peaches Davis, hit him for another single, he knew it was time to stop. He motioned to Hartnett to come to the mound.

"I think I oughtta call it a day," he said.

"Me, too," the catcher agreed. "That last pitch came up so slow Davis coulda written his name on the ball as it went by." He signaled Grimm in from the dugout. The manager walked to the mound slowly, waving for Larry French to come in from the bullpen.

"How's the wing?" he asked Dizzy.

"Stiff as a razorback's bristle."

"You did okay. Don't worry about it," Grimm said.

Dizzy walked off the mound slowly. The shoulder hurt, but he felt good inside. He had the notion that the Cubs were behind him all the way, no matter what happened to his arm.

With three days rest Grimm sent him back in, this time in Chicago, against his old teammates, the Cardinals. "I know how you feel going against them," Grimm said before the game. "You want to show 'em up. But don't press too hard. I got a couple of good guys in the bullpen. If you can go six, seven innings for me all season, we'll win a million."

"Charley, I promise I won't blow the game for you," Dizzy said soberly. "But I'm gonna try to go all the way. It means a lot to me."

Frisch picked as his pitcher one of the former Cubs, Curt Davis, as if to show Dizzy that the Cardinals had gotten the best of the trade. As the game began there was a lot of good-natured name-calling in both dugouts. The players on both teams recognized the mound duel as a kind of test.

But Dizzy was all business when the game began. His old mates could hardly believe that this was the same man. Their heckling went unanswered. Their jibes were ignored. They couldn't get a rise out of Dizzy. He was

153

too busy concentrating on his pitching. It wasn't like the old days when he knew he could just reach back and throw the ball right past a hitter. He knew now that craft and cleverness were his weapons.

Hartnett again led him along easily, calling for the fast ball only occasionally, but using it effectively after setting up the hitter with slow curves. Inning after inning Dizzy retired the Cardinals with ease, not striking out many but getting them on weak grounders and feeble pop-ups.

Owen reached him for a single in the third inning, and Stainback singled in the fourth. In the sixth, leading 2–0, he found himself in his first jam. With one out he walked Medwick. He got Frisch on a foul out, but Stainback beat out a slow roller to third. Johnny Mize, the powerful first baseman, was up next. Hartnett ran out to the mound. "I'm still trying to figure out this guy," he said. "Whatta you pitch him? You were with him last year."

Dizzy shrugged. "I never heard nobody say, and I never tried to figure him myself. Never thought I'd be pitchin' against him."

Hartnett grinned. "And I never thought I'd be catching you. Let's try him tight, on the fists." The red-faced catcher returned to his post and signaled for a fast ball.

Dizzy stretched, stopped, then tried to throw his hardest pitch of the day. He felt a burning strain at the back of his shoulder as he let go, but forgot it as Mize swung and popped the ball up for the third out.

The Cubs knocked across three more runs for him, giving him a 5–0 lead to work with. He retired three straight in the seventh, but he was feeling the pressure now. The shoulder stiffened and pained. The arm grew heavier with each pitch. Hartnett and Grimm both watched him carefully; they knew it would be good for his morale to finish, but it wouldn't be worth the price if he ruined his arm permanently.

Dizzy fought through the eighth inning, giving up just a walk, the strain beginning to show in the chalkiness of his face. Even the Cardinals were aware now of the strength of his determination. Their dugout was quiet as he strode stiffly to the mound to pitch the ninth inning. He got two outs, then Martin clipped him for the fourth Cardinal hit, a double. With Medwick at the plate the St. Louis dugout came alive again, chanting for the outfielder to drive Dizzy out of the box.

As teammates, there had never been much love lost between the two men. Now, as rivals for the first time, they faced each other across the diamond with all the barriers down.

Medwick cut savagely at the first pitch and fouled it off. The next one was outside and low for a ball. Dizzy came back with a fast ball on the inside for another ball. Then he broke off a sweeping curve just off the outside corner. A famous "bad ball" hitter, Medwick reached for the pitch as it broke, trying to slice it to right field. Instead he popped it foul along the first base line, where Rip Collins gathered it in for the final out.

The Cubs were jubilant in the clubhouse later. They pounded Dizzy on the back as though he had just pitched a World Series victory. He sat on a stool in front of his locker, grinning, easing his right arm painfully out of his sweatshirt.

"Diz looked like a million dollars today," manager Grimm beamingly told reporters in the clubhouse. "He didn't pitch his head off, but he bore down when he had to."

Catcher Hartnett was equally enthusiastic. "There's nothing the matter with that guy's arm," he said. "Sure it stiffened up on him in the late innings, but remember he only worked a few innings all through spring training. He'll loosen up with more work and warmer weather."

"You think you got another thirty-game season in you, Diz?" a sports writer asked. Recalling the expansive Dizzy of the old Gas House Gang days, he waited for the boastful reply.

But that Dizzy Dean was just a ghost haunting the Sportsman's Park clubhouse. "I don't know how much I'll win," he said modestly. "But I know I'll be doing my best."

With pitchers Lee and Bryant showing consistent winning form, a healthy Dizzy as a third starter would give the Cubs an unbeatable pitching trio. When the Giants followed the Cardinals into Wrigley Field, Grimm turned the threesome loose against Bill Terry's club. The New Yorkers were a floundering ball club, but with men like pitcher Carl Hubbell and the outstanding young right fielder Mel Ott in the line-up, they were apt to pull surprises. But the inspired Cubs helped Lee beat Hubbell, 9–4, driving the great pitcher from the box in the first inning; then Bryant beat Cliff Melton, 2–1.

156

In the third game Dizzy faced Hal Schumacher. The Giants drew first blood. With two men on in the second and two out, he got Wally Berger to hit to third, but the ball took a freak hop and bounded over Hack's head, scoring a run. Bearing down, he struck out rookie George Myatt to end the rally.

Two innings later, his teammates got the run back with interest. With one out Jurges and Herman singled and Cavaretta drove them both home with a triple.

Dizzy held the lead through the sixth inning. Then Ott doubled and Gus Mancuso singled him home with the tying run. Bartell hit a solid line drive right at Herman, who picked Mancuso off for a double play. Terry flied out to end the inning. But the chronic bursitis was beginning to make itself felt. On that last pitch to Terry, Dizzy had felt as though something had popped in his shoulder.

Due to bat first in the home half of the seventh inning, he picked out a bat and started to swing it. The pain made him stop suddenly. He thought about telling Grimm or Hartnett.

"Not yet," he said to himself grimly. "I gotta try one more inning. Besides, I want to get my licks at the plate."

He knew that with stiffness spreading through his right shoulder, a full swing would bring hot pain to the area. He waited out Schumacher's good curves, which went for called strikes, then picked out the "waste" pitch, an outside fast ball. He reached, flicked his wrists in a half-swing, and dropped the ball neatly into short right field for a single.

157

Grimm ruled out a sacrifice bunt on the next play. He didn't want to risk the possibility of Dizzy having to slide into second on a close play there. Instead he called for a hit-and-run. The hitter, Billy Herman, was a good bet to "get a piece of the ball"—that is, not strike out and trigger a double play on Dizzy, who would be committed to run for second on the pitch.

Herman swung on the first pitch and laced it just fair down the right field line—a perfect placement for a hit-and-run play, Dizzy rounded second, headed for third and ran right through third base coach Johnny "Lollipop" Corriden's stop sign.

Retrieving the ball in the right field corner, Ott fired a bullet to second baseman Alex Kampouris, who whirled toward third, expecting Dizzy to be holding there. Instead he saw the pitcher scrambling madly down the base line for home. Hurriedly Kampouris shifted and threw to burly Mancuso, blocking the plate. Dizzy slid in hard as the ball plunked into the catcher's big mitt. The umpire peered into the cloud of dust—and signaled safe!

Dizzy staggered to his feet, grinning, and trotted to the dugout. Above the din of the cheering crowd Grimm shouted to him: "I didn't call the bunt so you wouldn't have to slide. Now why'd you have to go and do a darn fool thing like that? You saw Corriden's signal to stop."

"I used to be the best base runner on the whole Gas House Gang," he said. "I wanted to see if'n I still could do it. Now we're leadin', ain't we?"

Grimm sighed. He had a vague inkling now of what Frisch must have gone through.

Schumacher choked off the rally. But Dizzy had a 3–2 lead to work with in the eighth inning. The shoulder was stiff and sore as he took his warm-up pitches. He wondered again whether he should take himself out of the game, but when the weak-hitting Kampouris settled into the batter's box he decided to stay as long as he possibly could.

He threw two slow curves to the second baseman, then a fast ball. Kampouris slammed it on a line to left center field for a double. That convinced Dizzy. It also convinced Grimm. He brought Russell in from the bullpen. The relief ace held the Giants scoreless in the final two innings, saving Dizzy's third straight victory.

The Cubs were leading the league now, the Pirates their only likely rivals; the Giants were too short on hitting, and the Cardinals were finding their trade doing little to help their pitching problems. Cub owner Phil Wrigley, the chewing-gum magnate, and manager Grimm patted each other on the back for thinking up the Cardinal trade.

Privately, Dizzy was not as elated. He alone knew that he was still pitching with an unnatural motion, favoring the shoulder, involuntarily flinching when he tried to throw the fast one, thus taking something off the pitch. But from Wrigley on down, the Cubs had been so fair to him, so considerate, he dreaded the thought that he might fail them. In his imagination sometimes he could hear Breadon and Rickey chortle as they discussed how they put one over on the Cubs, selling them a sore-armed pitcher for a small fortune and three players.

159

He was due to go against the Phillies in a few days. He would see. But he wouldn't quit.

The Philadelphians took the decision out of his hands. They hit him as though he was pitching batting practice for them, and when he had to leave in the third inning he was behind 5–1. His right arm felt like a shapeless lump of lead.

With Russell again in relief, the Cubs fought back. Dizzy represented something to them, a symbol of some kind. He was supposed to be the magic touchstone that would bring them the pennant. They also found that they liked him. They wanted him to win, as much for himself as for their own advantage. While their relief ace allowed just one more tally, they clubbed three Philadelphia hurlers for ten runs and a 10–6 victory. Russell was credited with the win, of course, but at least Dizzy didn't suffer the loss.

In the clubhouse later their spirits sank, however. On the rubbing table Dizzy was being probed and prodded by the club physician. The look on the doctor's face was not a cheerful one. "You'd better come into the office for a more thorough examination and X-rays," he said to the pitcher.

"Aw, Doc, it's just that ol' bursitis kickin' me in the shoulder again. It ain't no worse than gettin' kicked by one of them Army mules, which I'm used to. Why, once when I was in Fort Sam a mule—"

"Never mind," the doctor interrupted dryly. "This isn't the Army. There's a lot of money invested in your arm, not to mention what it means to your own liveli-

160

hood. I'm telling Grimm you're to be in my office at nine o'clock tomorrow morning."

The Cubs spent a restless night and morning waiting for the X-ray report. When it came the next afternoon it fell like a blow on the head. "Dizzy has what is called 'subdeltoid bursitis,' " the club physician said. "Apparently it's an aggravation of the condition he suffered last season. There isn't a thing we can do about it now except prescribe rest. Then later some conditioning exercises perhaps."

"How long a rest?" manager Grimm asked, afraid to hear the answer.

"Four weeks at least. He better not even try to throw a ball for two."

"Four weeks!" Grimm stifled a groan. "And how about after that. Will Diz be okay then at least?"

The physician hesitated before answering. "Bursitis is a treacherous condition. In Dizzy's case he has, if you'll pardon the technicalities, a lingering inflammation of the deltoid muscle at the point of insertion with the humerus —here," he said, pointing to a spot on the upper arm near the shoulder. "Now we can treat the pain of bursitis, offer prescriptions that will minimize its discomfort, but when a man has to pitch professional baseball with the condition"—the doctor shrugged expressively—"he's asking for trouble."

"You mean that it's really hopeless, that Dizzy will never be right again?" Grimm asked.

"I wouldn't say that at all. There's no injury to the bone. No calcification of the muscles. If he's lucky, with

161

a month's rest and careful conditioning he *could* come back as good as ever. But it's still an 'if.' "

Grimm was disconsolate. So was Dizzy. So were all the Cubs. Owner Phil Wrigley offered the only ray of sunshine. "At least we found this out now, when perhaps we can spare Dizzy for a few weeks. This way we'll have him back when we'll need him the most, when the pennant race really gets hot."

The four-week rest period passed. It turned into six weeks. Still Dizzy's arm remained inflamed and sore. The Cubs were beginning to feel panic. Though Lee and Bryant were pitching well, helped by French and Russell, another first-rate starter was needed. Without Dizzy it appeared impossible to catch the league-leading Pirates.

He tried to work his way back. He followed the doctor's conditioning orders precisely, slowly throwing a ball, first putting no effort behind it then gradually building up force. After just a few pitches the shoulder stiffened and locked. Further X-rays disclosed that the bursitis had set into the muscles back of the shoulder blade.

The All-Star game came and went without him, the first time in five years. Still he couldn't throw hard. Disgusted, he threatened to sue the Cardinals for a quarter of a million dollars. "This is all their fault," he said, in his first public outburst since joining the Cubs. "It all goes back last year to the All-Star game when I broke my toe. I didn't wanna play in that game anyways, but Frisch talked me into it. Then afterwards when I said I wasn't ready they made me pitch with a splint on my big toe. They ruined me, them Cardinals, working me to death all them years. And just to show everybody what I think of Mr. Wrigley, who is a fine gentleman, if'n I win the suit I'm gonna give him back that hundred eighty-five thousand he paid for me."

There was no lawsuit. Nobody for a moment thought there would be. Justified or not as any ballplayer might morally be, injuries and physical afflictions were the natural and accepted risks of the game, along with over-work, bad luck, unfair treatment and poor managing.

Still, for a little while at least the whole league was awakened by Dizzy's threat. For years he had provided the bulk of the exciting controversies. No one realized how much they had missed his extroverted clashes until now.

In mid-July Cub owner Wrigley asked Dizzy to pitch again. "We need you now," he said. "Even with a sore arm you're a better pitcher than half the major leaguers with good ones. Just do the best you can, that's all I expect."

Manager Grimm was optimistic again. "The latest X-rays show improvement," he said. "I think Diz's arm will get stronger with work. I bet he wins ten more games for me before the season's over."

Whatever Dizzy would do from then on, however, he would not do for Grimm. The manager was fired in mid-July, the feeling being that "Jolly Cholly" was too easy-going on players who needed a spur instead of a smile. In the tight, tough pennant race that loomed ahead, Wrigley wanted a stronger leader. He chose Gabby Hart-nett, and under the red-faced catcher's inspired urging,

163

the Cubs straightened out and took off after the league leaders.

As catcher and manager, Gabby was free to handle Dizzy exactly as he saw fit. With Wrigley's approval he held him out of the regular rotation, saving him for spots when he could be used to best strategic advantage. He slipped him in when rain bunched up a schedule, for example, forcing double-headers in close succession, putting a strain on the thin pitching staff. By holding him back, he was able to spot Dizzy against the teams known to have trouble hitting slow pitching. Harnett was in a position to know better than anybody, except Dizzy himself, how little the pitcher was able to put on the ball.

Dizzy won three more games and lost just one under Harnett's careful handling that summer. But as the pennant battle roared into its final month the bursitis crippled him again. Harnett was forced to bench him for two weeks. Dizzy fretted and paced the length of the dugout each day, frustrated by his uselessness.

By the middle of September the Pirates were so confident of winning the pennant that they ordered press buttons and an extra section built onto the grandstand. But the Cubs refused to fold in the stretch. They hung on, winning their games one by one, playing each day as it came.

Gradually, steadily, the Pittsburgh lead dwindled, until the issue remained to be settled, appropriately, by the two teams themselves in the final days of the season. Holding a slim-half-game lead by now, the Pirates managed a split of the first two games of the four-game climactic series, but Harnett himself won the next game with a ninth-inning home run, and for the first time in many weeks the Cubs led the league.

But there remained that final game to win. The Cubs were tired. They had played inspired ball for weeks, better ball than they had been expected to play. The pitching staff was badly overworked. That last, all-important game was going to be a wearisome one.

The clubhouse was quiet when manager Hartnett walked through the doors. The men were determined, but anxious. Who was Hartnett going to pitch? Which willing but weary-armed hurler would get the call?

Hartnett was not talking just yet. He changed into his uniform, extracted a big cigar from his jacket pocket before hanging it away in his locker, lit up carefully, then, puffing out a cloud of blue smoke he walked over to Dizzy and said, "Dean, you're the pitcher today."

"Fine," Dizzy said, not believing it for a moment.

Hartnett nodded and walked out to the dugout passage-way.

Dizzy continued to dress slowly, wondering vaguely why Hartnett had chosen to joke with him at that moment. Suddenly Larry French and Billy Herman burst in from the playing field.

"Hey, Diz," French said, "Hartnett says you're pitching today. That right?"

Dizzy stared at him. "Me? Well—well he said I was but I thought sure he was foolin'."

"No, he ain't kidding," Herman said. "He told us just

165

now. Ain't that great. You're just the guy we need out there today."

The enthusiasm of the two players was infectious. Anxious frowns were replaced by confident grins. "Ol' Diz'll knock 'em dead for us, won't you, Diz?" a player called out.

"They won't see you today, Diz," shouted another.

"You can do it, Diz."

"We'll get you the runs, Diz."

He was touched by his teammates' confidence, by the sudden flame of enthusiasm that was sparked by the knowledge that he would pitch for them today. He made up his mind that he would throw as hard as he could for as long as he could and let Hartnett know the second he felt he was finished.

But—the question hit him suddenly—just how hard could he throw now? He had hardly touched a ball in two weeks. The rest might have done him good; on the other hand, it might have helped not at all, perhaps even made his shoulder stiffer by disuse.

Well he would find out soon enough. He went out into the morning sunshine and began to warm up, very slowly. After ten minutes he walked into the dugout and sat down next to Hartnett. "Gabby, I can't throw hard enough to break a pane of window glass," he said.

Hartnett nodded. "I figured that. But in a spot like this, the pot boiling over, you're the man I want out there. Together we can do it. Go five, six innings. Then I can get French in there, even Lee. We gotta win this one, Diz."

166

"I'll pitch," Dizzy sighed. "But I better be the cleverest I ever have been today. 'Cause I got nothin' balls to throw. Jest nothin' balls."

It took the Pirates four innings to discover that what Dizzy was throwing were not his change-of-pace pitches, but the best he had. By that time the Cubs had given him a 2–0 lead he fought like a tiger to protect.

He may have been throwing "nothin' balls," as he called them, but he was throwing them to spots, controlling the pitches masterfully, moving the ball around on the hitters so they couldn't get set. He worked the corners, inside and out, slipping strikes just above the knees, getting the hitters to reach for tantalizingly slow curves that were hit into the dirt or popped into the air.

The pain in his shoulder was excruciating, but he forced himself to ignore it. His arm grew heavy and weary. He staggered through the sixth inning, the seventh, pitched out of trouble with two men on in the eighth. Finally there was just the last inning to go.

He couldn't make it. Two hits put the tying runs on first and third. Harnett signaled for Bill Lee to relieve and walked with Dizzy back to the dugout. "You did it." the catcher-manager said. "You did it, Diz. Lee'll hold 'em for you, don't worry."

For heart-stopping minutes it looked as though Lee could not save the game. Overanxious, he made his first pitch a wild one and a run scored. But he recovered his composure and held the Pirates back for the pennant-clinching victory.

167

In the clubhouse celebration that followed, Dizzy put his arm around Lee's neck and hugged him. "You saved it for me, Lee. You're a great man."

"No," Lee said. "You're the great one, Dizzy."

Nobody there denied it. Not even Dizzy.

14 ●●●●●●

The special world of sports in many ways is not so different from the ordinary world around it. In both worlds courage may often be admired more than talent, the lesser man loved and the better man hated, and adversity become the man more than success.

So it seemed to unfold in the life of Dizzy Dean. His peak years with the Gas House Gang were filled with bickering, fines and suspensions. He antagonized players, umpires, league executives and even some fans. He was loud and boastful. But that was Dizzy. It must be remembered that he played in an era when baseball was fought with spikes high and sharp and Leo Durocher's immortal motto: "Nice guys finish last!"

His first year with the Cubs changed much of all that. His fast ball was gone; his pitching arm in fact was gone. Subdued, grateful for the consideration shown him by the Cubs, he forced himself to pitch more on sheer courage than anything else—for indeed he had little else to pitch with. Suddenly, pleasantly, he found that so many of the same people who by word and in print had sniped at him for so many years, now hailed him. His stirring, crucial victory over the Pirates was acclaimed as one of the finest moments of his career.

The World Series of 1938 opened in Wrigley Field with the Yankees, American League winners for the third straight time, strong favorites over the Cubs. The National Leaguers had little to compare with Joe McCarthy's great aggregation. Ailing but still one of the best of all time, Lou Gehrig stood at first base. Joe Gordon was at second, Frank Crosetti at shortstop, Red Rolfe at third. The outfield was patrolled by Tommy Henrich, Joe DiMaggio and George Selkirk. Bill Dickey caught a staff headed by Red Ruffing, Lefty Gomez, Monte Pearson and Bump Hadley.

Two Yankee runs in the second inning decided the first game. With one out Gehrig walked and Dickey singled, Bill Lee got Selkirk to hit to second, but Herman let the ball go through, scoring Gehrig. Then Gordon singled Dickey home.

Ruffing lost one of the runs back in the third inning on a pair of singles sandwiched around a sacrifice, but that was all he gave away. The Yankees scored one more time for a 3–1 victory.

Again Hartnett called upon Dizzy. Lame-armed but strong in heart, he took the mound in the second game against one of the all-time great slugging teams in baseball history. The Yankees knew he had nothing on the ball, and they were waiting for him with their big bats.

After he had retired Crosetti, Rolfe and Henrich in order in the Yankee half of the first inning, the Cubs gave him a run with two hits off Gomez. But DiMaggio opened the second inning with a single and Gehrig walked.

Hartnett came out from behind the plate and walked to the mound. "I'm okay, I'm okay," Dizzy said, waving him back. Feeding Dickey slow curves and change-ups, he got the catcher to foul out. Selkirk he retired on a fly ball to Cavaretta. Then Joe Gordon hit an easy roller to the left side of the infield for what appeared to be an easy third out. But charging the ball at the same time Hack and Jurges bumped heads and fell to the grass. The ball bounced crazily through the gap and trickled into left field for a double, scoring both runners. Gomez grounded out, but the Yankees led, 2–1.

The Cubs, as though making amends for their carelessness, got the two runs back in the third inning. Hack and Herman singled, then, after a sacrifice bunt, Marty's double scored them.

Dizzy held on to that 3–2 lead with everything he had left. Calling on every bit of reserve skill and courage and strength, he completely mastered the great Yankee hitters for the next five innings. He was throwing his "nothin' ball," but the Yankees were pounding it into the ground and popping it up. Gehrig singled in the fourth but Dizzy got Dickey to bang into a double play. The partisan Chicago crowd cheered him loudly inning by inning as he mowed down the Yankees.

Selkirk opened the Yankee eighth with a single. Dizzy was tired now. He had given all of his head and his heart and what little remained of his arm—that flaming, aching

171

right arm that seemed to hang uselessly by his side between pitches.

Somehow he found enough strength to pitch to Gordon. The speedy young second baseman forced Selkirk at second but beat the double-play relay. Dizzy heaved a great sigh, opened his mouth wide and sucked in a great lungful of air. His uniform was black with perspiration. He could feel the drops trickling down his spine and the backs of his thighs. With the back of his glove he wiped the haze from his eyes and peered down for the sign from Hartnett. How many out? One. He was having trouble remembering.

A hiss of agony escaped his lips as he threw a slow curve to pinch-hitter Myril Hoag. It was good for a strike. Another slow curve—it was just about the only pitch he had. Hoag swung and bounced the ball to Hack, who threw to second for the force play. Two out. Crosetti up.

More slow curves to Crosetti. The Yankee shortstop, a pesky but not powerful hitter, suddenly lashed out at one of Dizzy's "nothin' balls" and hit it over the left field wall for a home run.

His back to home plate, Dizzy watched dazedly as the ball cleared the barrier. He realized that he was losing now, 4–3. He shook himself back to his task. The game wasn't lost yet. Red Rolfe was up. He had struck him out before. Well now he'd do it again just to show the Yankees the way it used to be.

Gritting his teeth he hurled a fast ball past Rolfe; then with two sweeping curve balls struck him out again.

That final, glorious effort took everything else out of

Dizzy. Henrich hit him for a single to start the ninth and DiMaggio hit his first pitch for a home run.

Sadly Hartnett walked out to the mound, took the ball from Dizzy's grasp and called in Larry French. There were tears in the eyes of many a fan, more than one hard-bitten sports writer and even a player or two as Dizzy, head hung low, his arms hanging helplessly, walked slowly back to the dugout.

He was followed every foot of the way by a wave of applause and cheers such as he had never heard in his life. In adversity he had gained more than all his many victories had ever brought him.

The next two games were hardly contests as Yankee power and pitching pushed the Cubs aside for a four-game sweep and the World's Championship. The outcome was hardly a surprise to the experts. As for disheartened Cub fans, they extracted what glory they could from the telling and retelling of how ol' Dizzy Dean almost beat the great Yankees with his heart and his "nothin' ball."

"Ol' Diz," as they were beginning to call him, was still only twenty-seven years old.

Often, as he looked back in later years, Dizzy thought that he would have been wise to hang up his glove right after that World Series game. It was in defeat a glorious moment, perhaps the most memorable of his career, certainly the most poignant. But he was only twenty-seven, and he hated to quit as a loser. So he lingered on, and the Cubs were good to him. He actually earned more salary winning a total of sixteen games for the Cubs than he did winning one hundred thirty-four with the Cardinals.

In 1939 he won six and lost four. He tried everything he could think of to bring his arm back to life. He saw dozens of doctors, tried an endless variety of pills, nostrums and injections. He tried rest and he tried exercise. Nothing worked.

Still, he wasn't too proud to try something new. He agreed in 1940 to return to the Texas League, to practice pitching sidearm, hoping that would help. He won eight and lost eight pitching sidearm in Tulsa, then returned to the Cubs to win the last three games of his career, and lose the last three games.

He was thirty years old when, in May of 1941, he asked the Cubs to let him quit. They had carried him and his useless arm long enough. But ever magnanimous with Dizzy, they refused to retire him. The new Chicago manager, Jim Wilson, was the same Wilson who, as star catcher for the Cardinals, helped him break into the big leagues in 1932. It was just nine years earlier, but so much had been packed into the short baseball life of his that it seemed more like twenty.

Wilson had too much sentimental attachment for Dizzy to let him retire. He hired him as a coach and even got him a raise in salary. Overwhelmed and for one of the few times in his life speechless, Dizzy accepted the job. "Boy, the Cubs sure have been good to me," was all he could say. But to Wilson and owner Wrigley the happy look on his face was more eloquent than the several hundred words he might have used in the old days.

Dizzy remained as a Cub coach for two months. Then an old Texas League comment about him came home to roost—and laid golden eggs.

It was while playing and bragging for Houston in 1931 that he finally annoyed a local sports writer into commenting, "That Dean is like a regular radio loudspeaker."

In July, 1941, that's about what he became—a regular radio loudspeaker. The Browns and Cardinals signed him to broadcast their home games over KWK in St. Louis.

On July 6, 1941, Dizzy hung up his baseball uniform for the last time. He left behind a record of 150 victories, 83 losses and a thousand legends.

15 ••••••

Considering what his career as a baseball pitcher was like, it was only to be expected that Dizzy's life as a sports announcer would claim its share of controversy. To begin with it was apparent that he was signed for his reputation as a pitcher and former Cardinal, not for any latent announcing talent he might have. Any such talent, it was quickly observed, would have been buried in any case under the torrent of ungrammatical gibberish that poured out of Dizzy in his rookie radio days.

He was bad. He either left the listener with yawning gaps of silence while he thought of something to say or let go a flow of meaningless chatter. He made technical mistakes, such as describing a pitcher as taking a full windup with men on base, and his attempts at interpreting strategy were halting and unconvincing. As a baseball man he knew, of course, what was happening on the field, but he had not yet learned how to channel his thoughts so that they would come smoothly from his tongue as he watched the scene.

What assets Dizzy did have at first were an overwhelming enthusiasm for the game, a vast store of tales about

176

his playing days, and a vast ignorance of the niceties and taboos of radio broadcasting. He was no cool, neutral broadcaster. He aired his opinions about everything; he rooted openly for the Cardinals; he salted his comments with language never heard before on radio.

The fans loved him, even when they couldn't follow him. He had trouble pronouncing names, so he called the players by the closest thing to their real one he could say. Kurowski became "Juroski." Musial he called "Moozell." Brecheen became "Burseen." Even a simple name like Cooper he pronounced "Cupper."

Informality was very definitely the tone of his broadcasts. He called out encouragement to the players, heckled the umpires. One time he leaned out of the broadcasting booth and yelled to Cardinal catcher Walker Cooper, "Look out there, Cupper! The hit-and-run's on!" Pittsburgh manager Al Lopez stepped out of his dugout and shook his fist angrily at the booth. The hit-and-run was indeed on, and Dizzy had tipped off the Cardinals to the signal.

Another day, in a close game, Cardinal pitcher Howie Pollet was working with the bases loaded and two out. "Watch it now, Pilot, watch it now!" Dizzy cautioned him. Then, when the ball was delivered, he got on the umpire. "Well what're you gonna call it, Barr? A strike! That's a good boy, Barr. You know," he commented to the listeners, "some of them umpires ain't bad at all, no sir."

As the months passed he was able to retain the color his comments provided and polish his delivery, at least

177

to the point where he actually followed the continuity of the ball game. The flavor of his Arkansas background and his maverick attitude soon made him a widely known, but sometimes widely criticized, sports commentator.

But he was irrepressible. During the war, for example, radio commentators were forbidden to mention the weather, presumably lest they give valuable information to potential enemy bombers. It seemed like one of the sillier rulings at the time, since weather conditions were not difficult to discover no matter where in the world. Dizzy obeyed the order as did everyone else, but found it difficult one day to explain to his listeners why a game had suddenly been called. He finally figured out a way without violating security. "I ain't allowed to tell you why the game was called, folks," he said, "but that ain't sweat drippin' down the pitcher's face."

During a Browns game one day pitcher Bob Muncreif threw an inside fast ball that made the batter hit the dirt. "Whew!" Dizzy commented. "That sure was a near one. Of course, you can't call it a duster 'cause in the American League they're not supposed to throw dusters. But they do throw 'em close once in a while."

In those days, when a team played away from home, the broadcasters would work in the home city, getting the play-by-play on a ticker, something like a stock-market ticker. The reports, of course, were sketchy, and so the announcers would fake in some action to fill the time. Dizzy hated this. Finally one day he became disgusted with the method. "Folks, we ain't gettin' this stuff the way we're handin' it out to you," he confided to his listeners. "They jest send a few words from the ball park, and we gotta imagine the rest. It's a lotta bunk!"

Between choruses of the "Wabash Cannonball," which he sang regularly as his favorite hillbilly song, and idle comments about his wife's delicious fried chicken, Dizzy gabbed merrily over the St. Louis airwaves for five years with little more than an occasional sniping by a radio columnist or local schoolteacher. But in 1946 the Missouri Schoolteachers Association complained formally to the Federal Communications Commission that Dizzy's errors of grammar and syntax were having bad effects on their pupils.

The teachers cited recent and repeated transgressions:
"Slaughter slud safely into second."
"Marion throwed Reiser out at first."
"The runners held their respectable bases."
"Musial looks hitterish up there at the plate."
"Don't fail to miss tomorrow's game."

The teachers didn't stand a chance against the avalanche of mail that poured in to defend Dizzy. The people liked the way he broadcast; he knew what he was talking about, and he said it colorfully, which to a great many people was more important than his saying it grammatically.

Dizzy's only comment was, "What do they want me to say—slidded instead of slud?"

He lived in Dallas now, had a farm where he raised Hereford steers, and owned some good real estate in Texas that added to his income. Brother Paul was settled nicely, operating the Lubbock, Texas, club of the West Texas–New Mexico Baseball League; brother Elmer and Pa Dean lived comfortably in nearby Garland.

But just to show some of the young players that he still had a little something on the ball, he talked the Browns into letting him pitch against the White Sox on the last day of the 1947 season. The game meant nothing in the final standings.

Dizzy felt strange in baseball flannels again, but he pitched four good innings, giving up just three hits. He would have liked to have pitched more, but running out a single in the third inning he pulled a leg muscle that caused him to leave an inning later.

"But say," he said afterward, a calculating glint in his eye, "I bet I still could get enough fellers out to earn my keep as a relief pitcher."

That fall he made his one and only excursion into football broadcasting. The game proved to be beyond his understanding. He referred to the officials as "those guys wearing striped pajamas," and called the head linesman "a guy with a gun who must be low on ammunition or a poor shot, because I ain't never seen him hit nobody." He refused a second such assignment. "Football is too rough for me," he said. "I was hurt three times during the broadcast, and the only play I called right was the kickoff."

The Yankees hired Dizzy for their TV broadcasts in 1950, and for many years he salted the New York air with his special and colorful style until he switched to the "Game of the Week" broadcast, where he is today.

Hollywood made a film of his life in 1952, *Pride of St. Louis,* in which Dan Dailey portrayed him. And in 1953 he was elected to Baseball's Hall of Fame, an honor reserved only for the immortals in baseball history.

He was the last pitcher in the major leagues to win thirty games. The closest anyone has come to his record are Hal Newhouser, who won twenty-nine games in 1944 for the Detroit Tigers, and Robin Roberts, who had twenty-eight victories in 1952 for the Philadelphia Phils. In the five good seasons Dizzy played before the All-Star injury that curtailed his career, he won 121 games, an average of 24 victories a season. He was one of the best-hitting pitchers in baseball and, even on the Gas House Gang, was considered an exceptional base runner.

At a recent Old-Timers game in New York, reminiscing with some of the sports writers who had seen him come up as a fresh rookie from the Texas League, Dizzy accurately and modestly offered an estimate of his own abilities.

"I may not have been the greatest pitcher ever in baseball," he drawled, "but I sure was amongst them."

Nobody disagrees.

181

JAY HANNA (DIZZY) DEAN

Height, 6'3" Weight, 202 Threw and batted right-handed

Year.	Club.	League.	G.	IP.	W.	L.	Pct.	H.	R.	ER.	SO.	BB.	ERA.
1930—St. Joseph	Western	32	217	17	8	.680	204	118	89	134	77	3.69
1930—Houston	Texas	14	85	8	2	.800	62	31	27	95	49	2.82
1930—St. Louis	Nat.	1	9	1	0	1.000	3	1	1	5	3	1.00
1931—Houston	Texas	41	304	26	10	.722	210	71	53	303	90	1.53
1932—St. Louis	Nat.	46	286	18	15	.545	280	122	105	191	102	3.30
1933—St. Louis	Nat.	48	293	20	18	.526	279	113	99	199	64	3.04
1934—St. Louis	Nat.	50	312	30	7	.811	288	110	92	195	75	2.65
1935—St. Louis	Nat.	50	324	28	12	.700	326	128	112	182	82	3.11
1936—St. Louis	Nat.	51	315	24	13	.649	310	128	111	195	53	3.17
1937—St. Louis	Nat.	27	197	13	10	.565	200	76	59	120	33	2.70
1938—Chicago	Nat.	13	75	7	1	.875	63	20	15	22	8	1.80
1939—Chicago	Nat.	19	96	6	4	.600	98	40	36	27	17	3.38
1940—Chicago	Nat.	10	54	3	3	.500	68	35	31	18	20	5.17
Major League Totals			315	1961	150	83	.644	1915	773	661	1154	457	3.03

WORLD'S SERIES RECORD

Year.	Club.	League.	G.	IP.	W.	L.	Pct.	H.	R.	ER.	SO.	BB.	ERA.
1934—St. Louis	Nat.	3	26	2	1	.667	20	6	5	17	5	1.73
1938—Chicago	Nat.	2	8⅓	0	1	.000	8	6	6	2	1	6.75
World's Series Totals			5	34⅓	2	2	.500	28	12	11	19	6	2.88

Index

Adams, Sparky, 100, 103
Alexander, Grover Cleveland, 13
American League, 68-69, 105, 125-26, 144-45, 170
Arkansas, 9, 13, 22, 178
Associated Press, 118
Athletics, Philadelphia, 67-69, 86
Averill, Earl, 144
Auker, Elden, 105, 114-15

Baer, Max, 118
balk rule, the, 137
Barr, George, 137-38
Baseball Writers Association, 118
Belleville, Illinois, 138
Bellevue-Stratford Hotel, 88
Benge, Ray, 98
Berger, Wally, 157
bird dog, in relation to baseball, explanation of, 44
Black Yankees, 121
Blades, Ray, 62
Blanton, Cy, 129
Boston Braves. See Braves, Boston
Boston, Massachusetts, 88, 146
Bottomley, Jim, 101
Boyle, Ralph, 98
Bradenton, Florida, 65, 123
Braves, Boston, 90-91, 125, 143
Breadon, Sam, 78, 92, 123-25
Bridges, Tommy, 107, 111-12
Brooklyn Bushwicks, 121

Brooklyn, New York, 98, 121, 139
Brought, Sergeant Johnny, 30-31, 32-35, 38-46, 50-52
Browns, St. Louis, 175, 180
Bryant, Clay, 152, 156, 162
bursitis, 147, 160-61
Bush, Guy, 80

Campbell, Bill, 81
Cardinals, St. Louis, 43-44, 53, 60-70, 72-73, 74-104, 105-18, 122-24, 128, 135-39, 143-51, 153-55, 159, 162, 175, 177
Carleton, Tex, 87, 108, 129, 152
Cavaretta, Phil, 152, 157, 171
Chicago Cubs. See Cubs, Chicago
Chicago, Illinois, 121, 126, 153
Chickalah, Arkansas, 9
Cincinnati, Ohio, 151
Cochrane, Mickey, 68-69, 105, 113-15, 117
Collins, Rip, 86, 89, 96, 101, 106, 108, 115, 134, 151, 152
Columbus club, 73, 80, 84
Comorosky, Adam, 102
Cooper, Walker, 177
Corriden, Johnny "Lollipop," 158
Critz, Hughie, 75, 96
Crosetti, Frank, 170, 172
Crosley Field, 151, 152
Crowder, General, 105-06

185

Dean, Monroe (father), 11-15, 16-19, 24, 35-37, 52, 59, 78, 180
Dean, Mrs. (mother), 11-12
Dean, Patricia (wife), 71-72, 120-21, 123, 136. *See also* Nash, Patricia
Dean, Paul (brother), 12, 13-14, 16-18, 21, 35-37, 52, 59, 72-73, 80, 84, 87, 91-93, 96, 98-99, 100, 107-08, 112-14, 120-22, 123, 129, 134-35, 149-50, 179-80
"Deanville", 123
DeLancey, Bill "Kayo," 87, 101, 103, 106-07, 112-13, 115, 129, 134
Demaree, Frank, 81
Dennis, Ralph, 9-10
Derringer, Paul, 122
Detroit, Michigan, 92, 112
Detroit Tigers. *See* Tigers, Detroit
Dickey, Bill, 170-71
DiMaggio, Joe, 170-71, 173
DiMaggio, Vince, 90-91
Dodgers, Brooklyn, 86, 98-102, 147, 181
Dozier, Grace, 95, 99
Durocher, Leo, 79-80, 85, 86, 95, 96-97, 99, 108-09, 112-15, 117-19, 129, 147, 169

Ebbets Field, 139
England, 118

Federal Communications Commission, 179
First Presbyterian Church, 138
Fitzsimmons, Freddie, 96
Florida, 65, 136
Fort Sam Houston, 19-24, 25-52
Fort Worth team, 72
Fox, Pete, 105, 107, 110-11
Foxx, Jimmy, 68

French, Larry, 152, 153, 162, 165, 173
Frick, Ford, 138-43
Frisch, Frank, 62-63, 79-81, 84-85, 86-88, 92-93, 99, 100-02, 106-19, 128-31, 135-37, 139, 143-48, 153-54
Fullis, Chuck, 116

Garland, Texas, 180
Gas House Gang, 85-104, 105-18, 129-33, 134, 136, 146-50
Gehrig, Lou, 170-71
Gehringer, Charley, 105, 107, 109, 112-13
Gelbert, Charley, 62
Giants, New York, 75-76, 78, 85, 86, 89-90, 91, 95, 96-102, 131-33, 135, 137-38, 143, 156-59
Gomez, Lefty, 170-71
Gonzalez, Mike, 116
Gordon, Joe, 170-72
Goslin, Goose, 105, 107, 110, 113
Greenberg, Hank, 105-08, 110-11, 114, 117-18
Grimes, Burleigh, 62, 81, 83
Grimm, Charley, 82-83, 151-63

Hack, Stan, 152, 157, 171-72
Hadley, Bump, 170
Hafey, Chuck, 62
Hahn, Frank, 82
Haines, Pop, 87
Hall of Fame, 181
Hallahan, Wild Bill, 62, 65, 67, 87, 107, 134
Hartnett, Gabby, 151-53, 154-56, 163-67, 170-73
Hendrick, Harv, 82
Henrich, Tommy, 170, 172
Herman, Billy, 81, 152, 157-58, 165, 170-71

187